**Salamis in Cyprus**

NEW ASPECTS OF ANTIQUITY
*Edited by Sir Mortimer Wheeler*

# Salamis in Cyprus

## Homeric, Hellenistic and Roman

*Vassos Karageorghis*

*17 Colour Plates*
*128 Monochrome Plates*
*33 Line Drawings*

THAMES AND HUDSON

This edition © Thames and Hudson 1969

All Rights Reserved. No part of this publication
may be reproduced, stored in a retrieval system, or
transmitted, in any form or by any means, electronic,
mechanical, photocopying, recording or otherwise,
without prior permission of the Publishers.

First Published 1969

Filmset in Great Britain by Keyspools Ltd, Golborne, Lancs
Text printed in Great Britain by Fletcher and Son Ltd, Norwich
Bound in Great Britain by Richard Clay (The Chaucer Press) Ltd, Bungay, Suffolk
500 39006 1

# Contents

|     | GENERAL EDITOR'S PREFACE | 7 |
| --- | --- | --- |
|     | FOREWORD | 11 |
| I   | THE SITE OF SALAMIS | 13 |
| II  | SALAMIS AT THE END OF THE BRONZE AGE | 20 |
| III | THE AGE OF EXUBERANCE: THE NECROPOLIS IN THE EIGHTH AND SEVENTH CENTURIES | 23 |
|     | *Tomb 1* | 25 |
|     | *Tomb 2* | 28 |
|     | *Tomb 47* | 50 |
|     | *'Tomb' or 'Prison of St Catherine' (Tomb 50)* | 54 |
|     | *Tomb 3* | 67 |
|     | *Tombs 19 and 31* | 72 |
|     | *Tomb 79* | 76 |
|     | *Tomb 80* | 98 |
|     | *Cellarka* | 99 |
|     | *Pyre A* | 120 |
|     | *Pyre L* | 120 |
|     | *Pyre Q* | 120 |
|     | *Tomb 105* | 121 |
|     | *Tomb 84* | 127 |
|     | *Tomb 10* | 128 |
|     | *Tomb 23* | 130 |
|     | *Infant Burial* | 149 |
| IV  | A KING'S CENOTAPH | 151 |
| V   | THE CITY SITE | 165 |

| | | |
|---|---|---|
| VI | SALAMIS – CONSTANTIA | 197 |
| | NOTES | 199 |
| | SELECT BIBLIOGRAPHY | 205 |
| | LIST OF ILLUSTRATIONS | 207 |
| | INDEX | 211 |

# General Editor's Preface

SALAMIS OF CYPRUS, legendary foundation of Teucer, son of Telamon king of the Greek Salamis and brother of Ajax, was for a millennium after the Trojan War the chief city of Cyprus. Recently French archaeologists have lighted upon some of its early vestiges amidst the sand and scrub on the coast north of Famagusta, and, as so often, fact and legend appear to have a measure of mutual consistency. But the primary purpose of this book is to present a very remarkable series of Salaminian tombs which belong for the most part to a somewhat later age, and have since 1957 been excavated with impeccable skill by Dr P. Dikaios and by his successor Dr V. Karageorghis.

Though a majority of these tombs have been sadly plundered through the centuries, their careful excavation has recovered more than a fragmentary catalogue of craftsmanship and custom. They are above all a vivid commentary upon the culture of the age of the Homeric epics as we have them: less of the age to which those epics ostensibly relate than of the age in which they were ultimately written down.

The differences in time and culture between those ages are of course appreciable and have long offered happy employment to a multitude of scholars. The siege of 'Priam's Troy', equated with Professor Blegen's 'Troy VIIA', is agreeably ascribed in general accordance with literary tradition and modern archaeology to the half-century before 1200 BC. But the adaptation of the Phoenician alphabet which at last enabled the Homeric epics to be written down in something like their present form does not appear to have been fully developed until the middle of the eighth century BC. (A tolerable hexameter scratched upon a pot of about 725 BC from the Dipylon cemetery at Athens is the first Greek verse at present known.) The interval between the two Homeric phases – as they may be called – was a long one, perhaps five centuries, and was fraught with possibilities of change.

One of the differences which emerged during the interval related to burial-custom. Archaeology tells us that the Mycenaean Greeks whom Agamemnon led against Troy almost invariably buried their dead intact. The Homeric rite on the other hand was cremation. And so, in the eighth–seventh centuries BC was the partially contemporary and comparable rite in the Salamis cemetery as now revealed by Dr Karageorghis. True, there is sometimes a tendency to overstress the significance of a divergence of this kind. Down to the present day, inhumation and cremation have on occasion subsisted side by side in the same community. Nevertheless, the somewhat precise insistence of the leaders of the Mycenaeans upon one rite, and of their epic and Salaminian counterparts (if such they may be called) upon the other is a deviation worthy of a moment's consideration in the wider context of historic values.

Without anticipating Dr Karageorghis's very clear descriptions and commentaries in any detail, the main points may briefly be stated as follows:

(i) From amidst the tangled controversies which have bemused the attribution and chronology of the aristocratic *tholos* tombs of the Mycenaean world, it is now fair to ascribe some proportion of them to the thirteenth century BC, the century of the Trojan episode. They consisted typically of a domed burial-vault approached by a dromos or passage, and were used for multiple and richly equipped interments. Relatively few of the minutiae however have survived subsequent looting.

(ii) The standard Homeric burial of a Greek hero is of course that of Patroklos in the twenty-third book of the *Iliad*. The funeral took place on the battlefield, and no elaborate tomb is therefore to be expected; that was indeed reserved explicitly for later construction. But the main procedure is clear and ample. The dead man on his bier was placed upon the summit of a great pyre, surrounded by the carcasses of cattle and sheep and amphorae containing honey and oil. For good measure, Achilles added four 'high-necked' horses and two of the dead man's dogs. Further, carried away by emotion, he did

*General Editor's Preface*

what even the heroic poet describes as 'an evil deed': he slew a dozen Trojan prisoners of noble birth, and then at last set a light to the whole macabre accumulation, the while he poured libations on the flames from a two-handled cup of gold. Thereafter he gave orders for the ashes of Patroklos to be carefully separated and to be sealed in a golden vase beneath a temporary mound, which was forthwith raised within a circular stone revetment.

(iii) Points of contact between both of these variants and the remarkable Salaminian dromos-tombs described in the present book are not lacking, and the author is careful to note them. The tombs consist normally of a rectangular chamber roofed with flat slabs and approached by a revetted dromos. With rare and uncertain exceptions, the successive burials are by cremation; the burnt bones might be wrapped in cloth and enclosed in a bronze cauldron or an amphora. The actual burning took place in the dromos, into which the hearse and/or a chariot had been drawn by horses or asses, subsequently sacrificed on the spot in circumstances vividly reconstructed by the excavator. Ranged along the walls, lines of amphorae had contained organic substances which may well on analysis turn out to include the honey and oil of the Homeric scene; in fact, one of the jars bears a painted inscription, 'of olive oil', in the Cypriote syllabary. It may be that in one instance an echo of Homer's sacrificed Trojans is to be recognized in a number of unburnt human skeletons – one at least of them bound hand and foot – incorporated in the filling which barred access into the dromos and completed the ceremony of burial. Lastly, the whole complex was covered by an earthen mound which might culminate in a beehive construction of sun-dried bricks suggesting, as the anthor observes, 'a remnant of a Mycenaean tradition in tomb architecture'.

Here it is reasonable to suppose that we have indeed a lingering ghost of Mycenaean ritual, with inhumation replaced by cremation as in the Homeric version. The question remains, How in the eighth century BC did this ritual travel to Cyprus, and in what circumstances had it changed from inhumation to cremation? These are not mere matters of pedantic curiosity. Did we know the answers, we should also know a great deal more of the significant history of the eastern Mediterranean in the mobile and formative eighth–seventh centuries than we know at present. Guesses are easy, but they remain guesses. The first of them must be based upon the familiar Greek *diaspora* across the eastern Mediterranean and beyond both before and after 700 BC, no doubt planting Greek traditions and innovations – Greek saws and modern instances, the latter including the practice of cremation which somewhere about 1100 BC those shadowy 'Dorians' seem to have imposed upon the Greek world. A rite which incidentally was particularly apt to an era of restless migration.

It may be, then, that in this Cypriote enclave we have a surviving glimpse of the sort of environment in which the Homeric scribes were working along the eastern fringe of the Aegean in the early days of classical Greek literacy. But the interest of the Salaminian tombs does not end there. Dr Karageorghis's examination of them will show something of the extent to which Cyprus was at this time not merely an outpost of the western Greek world but was likewise a point of entry for the Levant and its Egypto-Assyrian contacts. Today two of the treasures of the Cyprus Museum at Nicosia are a cleverly reconstructed throne and bed from the dromos of Tomb 79 enriched with carved ivory plaques, whilst other furniture from the same and similar deposits retained traces of silver veneer. The author is reminded of the ivory and silver chair of Penelope on the one hand and of the rich furniture of the Assyrian palaces on the other. Its geographical position and the lure of its mineral wealth combined to make Cyprus in this lively era a focus of the cosmopolitan craftsmanship which, with varying local bias, then characterised Eurasian civilization between the Tigris, the Nile and the Aegean.

Of a different kind is the very remarkable cenotaph identified as that of the last king of Salamis, Nicocreon, who with his family committed suicide in 311 BC rather than surrender to Ptolemy. The monument, with statues of unbaked clay, had been burnt in a pyre which had hardened and so preserved some of the sculptures and had subsequently been covered with a mound. This and much else are dealt with by Dr Karageorghis, whose book covers a wide range of interest and implies a background of highly accomplished archaeological technology.

MORTIMER WHEELER

# Foreword

Fifteen years of excavations at Salamis have brought to light enough archaeological material for an impressive series of books. The present writer, who has been associated with these excavations throughout their duration, does not claim to offer in this volume a comprehensive picture of all that they have revealed. On the city site the excavations of the complex public buildings is not yet completed, and therefore no detailed architectural account could be undertaken at this stage, except in broad general outlines. The numerous statues and inscriptions found during the excavations are not even summarily described; reference is made to them only in their historical and artistic contexts, and the specialist reader may be referred to the publications which describe them in detail[1] and which have already appeared or are in preparation.

In the necropolis the first phase of the excavations was completed in 1967.[2] The several thousand objects which have been registered from these excavations are still being cleaned and mended, and their study may take a number of years. About one hundred and fifty tombs have been excavated in the necropolis, and of these only six have so far been fully published.

In spite of this, however, the present volume should be considered neither as too preliminary an account nor as superfluous. Fifteen years of excavations[3] have helped to gather an impressive amount of archaeological information about Salamis leading to conclusions which have a bearing not only on Salamis itself but also on Cyprus as a whole.

No attempt has been made to reconstruct the history of Salamis by repeating what is already known from literary, epigraphic and other sources. The only purpose of this book is to emphasize the significance of recent discoveries at a site which was previously excavated to a large extent inadequately and unscientifically, and to demonstrate some new aspects of the archaeology of Salamis such as the monumentality of its tombs and the character of burial-customs hitherto unknown in Cyprus. Opportunity will be taken to describe objects like chariots and horse-gear, many of which are new finds occurring for the first time in Mediterranean archaeology. In one way and another the necropolis is well worthy of independent presentation.

The tombs, especially in the 'royal' part of the necropolis, baffle over-all classification. Each is liable to exhibit its own architectural and other peculiarities, and to demand somewhat detailed description. Some of the distinctive features, especially those connected with funerary rites, are of importance for the new aspect of the antiquity of Salamis which will emerge out of the contents of this book, namely its role as a stepping-stone between the Aegean and the Orient.

The city of Salamis, being the easternmost outpost of Hellenism, served throughout its history as a cultural and mercantile link between the Greek world and the Near East, a role which characterizes also the island of Cyprus as a whole. 'Homeric' funerary customs mingled with chariots and tomb-gifts of an Assyrian and Phoenician character, East Greek pottery and epitaphs for Phoenicians found side by side, all combine to support this claim.

The cenotaph of King Nicocreon, which is described in some detail, constitutes a direct link with the city's history and may be considered as of outstanding importance both in its architecture and in the remarkable character of the objects which were found on its funerary pyre.

It is true that the Roman and later remains of the city are not of the same standard of importance as the necropolis. Yet they demonstrate the continuing greatness of Salamis over a period of nearly two millennia.

# I

# The Site of Salamis

The region round the bay of Salamis, on the east coast of Cyprus, is one of the most favoured in the whole island. A large Late Bronze Age city, near the village of Enkomi, flourished from the seventeenth to the eleventh century BC[1] to be succeeded by Salamis which became the capital city of Cyprus for more than one thousand years. It is within the same region that Famagusta prospered during the Medieval period, and in modern times the new town of Famagusta has become one of the most thriving of the whole island. The hinterland of this region, the Mesaoria Plain, is one of the richest in Cyprus. The marshy region around the harbour offered the necessary supply of salt which was indispensable for the survival and growth of a town. The well protected bay offered natural harbours which were well exploited from the Late Bronze Age down to the present day. Finally, the geographical position of the region with the Syro-Palestinian coast, indeed the whole Near East, spreading in front of it at a distance less than one hundred miles favoured the harbour towns which developed here into important commercial centres, as the easternmost outpost of the Greek world, open to the cultures and to the wealth of the Orient.

Already in the fourteenth century BC the Late Bronze Age town of Enkomi received the first Mycenaean merchants from the Aegean, who used it as a base for their trade with the Near East; at the end of the thirteenth century the same town saw the first Achaean colonists establishing themselves on its soil and thus introducing Western culture to a land which was hitherto in all respects within the oriental sphere of influence. When Enkomi was succeeded by Salamis in the eleventh century BC the process of Westernization was accelerated, and soon this town became one of the most renowned of the Greek world often playing an important role in Greek politics especially during the heyday of Hellenic culture, in the fifth and fourth centuries BC.[5]

Salamis, however, shared the destiny of the rest of Cyprus during the successive occupations by the various dominant powers of the Near East, Assyrians, Egyptians and Persians. But political domination from outside did not always mean internal cultural decline. By preserving the essence of their Hellenic heritage on the one hand and accepting on the other hand new artistic and cultural ideas from the world of the Orient, the Salaminians created, during the period of oriental domination (mainly the eighth to sixth centuries BC) a robust culture, equal in quality and vitality to the Aegeo-oriental culture which developed at Enkomi in the fourteenth and thirteenth centuries BC from the contact of the Mycenaeans with Syria and Palestine. If to the term 'Hellenistic' one is prepared to give a wider meaning, one that denotes the expansion of the Hellenic culture in the Orient, whether in the Late Bronze Age or in the Archaic period, or during the Hellenistic period proper (third to second centuries BC), then we may legitimately accept Salamis and its predecessor Enkomi as the major centres of the 'Hellenizing' movement through which the Western culture of the Aegean was renewed and recovered strength for survival.[6]

A general characteristic of the material culture of Salamis throughout the first millennium BC, as demonstrated by recent archaeological discoveries, is the combination of wealth and exuberance. There may be a deeper reason for this which is not simply the outcome of prosperity. In the seventh century BC the kings of Salamis were buried in monumental tombs with fabulously luxurious burial gifts to equal the pomp and wealth of their Assyrian overlords.[7] In the fifth to fourth centuries BC the king of Salamis, Evagoras I, struck gold coins for the first time in order to demonstrate that he was not inferior to the Great King of Persia. This attitude may not mean simply slavish imitation but may be the result of a psychological reaction in the confrontation of East and West; an assertion of the pride, dignity and equality of the

*The Site of Salamis*

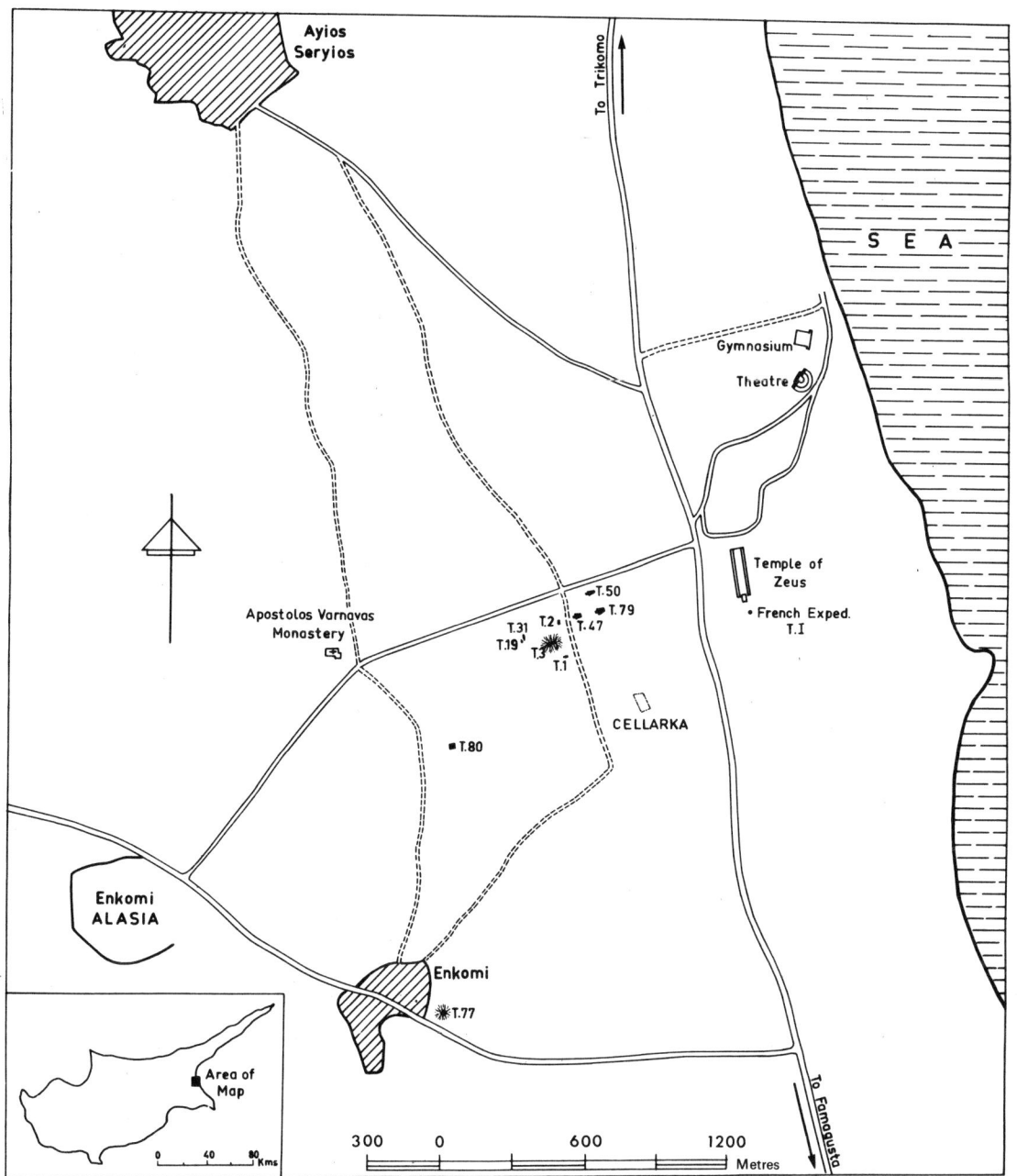

1   *Plan of the site of Salamis showing the city site on the right, along the sea, with all the hitherto uncovered monuments; to the left extends the necropolis with its 'royal' tombs*

*Salamis*

*Fig. 1*

indigenous culture of Salamis *vis à vis* that of the powerful Orient. It is not surprising, therefore, that the recent excavations in the necropolis of Salamis have not only demonstrated the extent to which the Salaminians persisted in the religious and burial customs of their forefathers, but also brought to light material wealth which in quality and style can be rivalled only by the best which the Near East may offer. In the contemporary world of scholarship, where the interrelations between the Orient and the Occident constitute a fascinating and crucially important element, Salamis thus offers a new aspect of antiquity well worthy of investigation.[8]

The ancient site of the city of Salamis covers an area of about one square mile extending along the sea shore, north of the estuary of the river Pedieos. It lies about five miles north of Famagusta, and two miles north-east of the Late Bronze Age site near the village of Enkomi. The whole area of the city site is a flat plain, now planted as a State forest with mimosas, pine trees and eucalyptus. The necropolis of Salamis, occupying an area of about two square miles, extends mainly outside the forest, over a cultivated plain, with its western border near the monastery of St Barnabas; the villages of Enkomi and Ayios Serghios form the southern and northern limits of the necropolis respectively. This is the largest ancient necropolis in the island, comprising tombs from the eleventh century BC down to the seventh century AD.

The Arab invasions of the seventh century AD put an end to the life of the ancient city of Salamis. Traces of the fire which destroyed the city are still visible on the sandstone surface of the walls of the newly excavated public buildings, and in the thick layers of ashes which are mixed with fallen debris throughout the city site. For several centuries afterwards squatters lived among its ruins. (Lusignan coins and medieval structures are to be found near the surface.) These squatters must have been attracted by the building material provided by the ruined buildings. Three kilns for gypsum have so far been found within the area of the recently uncovered Gymnasium and Theatre. At the Venetian Land-Gate of medieval Famagusta an inscribed statue base from the Gymnasium of Salamis is built in the wall, and several other architectural fragments of marble and granite (columns, capitals, cornices) may be seen adorning the buildings of the medieval successor of Salamis, not to mention the sandstone blocks with which the churches and the walls of Famagusta were built. Strong north-easterly winds soon covered the abandoned remains of the buildings of Salamis with blown sand, and thus preserved some of them to their original height, though the pillage of stone continued down to the second half of the twentieth century.

Travellers and scholars of the nineteenth century described the site of Salamis as 'thickly overgrown with thistles and tall weeds, which, together with the sand, render the task of inspecting it very difficult' (L. Palma di Cesnola). The remains of the city were nevertheless challenging, and the nineteenth-century British scholar D. G. Hogarth, travelling in Cyprus in 1889 wrote: 'On the landward side is a hideous chaos of stone, squared and unsquared, marble and granite shafts, fragments of cornices and capitals, but hardly a clear trace of any one building. There are, however, two places in this wilderness where I longed to set a few diggers to work.'[9] This temptation, however, was not Hogarth's alone. About ten years earlier Luigi Palma di Cesnola, an American Brigadier-General of Italian birth, acting as American consul to Cyprus, 'spent large sums of money' as he himself informs us, 'at this place on three different occasions, but with no result in any way satisfactory'.[10] His brother, Alexander Palma di Cesnola, also excavated at Salamis, but complains that he found nothing of importance. He no doubt came across the remains of late structures of the Early Christian period: 'I have many times hoped', he writes, 'to find a famous temple or other remains ... but all of these visions ended in nothing except foundations of common buildings.'[11]

Looting in the necropolis of Salamis started even earlier, and on a much larger scale, than on the city site. The villagers of nearby Enkomi and Ayios Serghios, on their own at first and later employed by the Cesnola brothers, devastated hundreds of tombs which could easily be detected just below the surface. The 'innumerable and precious pieces of jewellery' which were brought to light from these tombs had already impressed the medieval travellers; these, especially the scholars, were also fascinated by the name of Salamis as a city founded by Teucer, a hero of the Trojan war, governed by King Evagoras, who was praised by the Greek orator Isokrates, and as the birthplace of St Barnabas.[12]

The site of Salamis was 'rediscovered' during the early years of the British occupation of the island. The German scholar Dr Max Ohnefalsch-Richter, who was employed by the British administration to plant a forest in order to stabilize the sand-dunes over the site, came across ancient remains, some of which he excavated himself. He also carried out excavations in the necropolis.[13]. More tombs were excavated by Kitchener and Hake for the South Kensington Museum (now the Victoria and Albert Museum) in 1882.[14] Extensive excavations were carried out during 1890 and 1891 by a British expedition which opened trenches all over the city site but without completing the excavation of any building.[15] In 1896 another British mission excavated tombs in the necropolis with more or less negative results.[16] None of these excavations were ever published properly, and apart from the significance of some of the material which was found in them, and which is now scattered in various museums of the world, they added very little to our knowledge of the archaeology of Salamis.

In 1924–5 and 1933 excavations on a very limited scale were carried out by G. E. Jeffery and Joan du Plat Taylor respectively, mainly in early Christian buildings.[17]

It was in 1952, however, that the Department of Antiquities started large-scale excavations at the city site. These have continued up to the present day,[18] and in 1962 the Department of Antiquities undertook the systematic excavation of the necropolis, the first phase of which was completed in 1967.

The result of these excavations at the city site showed beyond doubt that here, at the northern extremity, there were only late Hellenistic and Roman remains, and that the remains of the earlier city should be sought further to the south. The search for the earlier remains of Salamis was intensified after the outstanding results achieved in the excavations of the first tombs of the archaic period excavated in the necropolis. With this object in view the Department of Antiquities granted a permit to a French expedition from the University of Lyon to investigate the south sector of Salamis. The first campaign was carried out in 1964 and the excavations have continued uninterruptedly and rewardingly for two seasons every year.[19]

# II

# Salamis at the End of the Bronze Age

There was a time when scholars referring to Late Bronze Age Salamis meant the well-known Bronze Age site of Enkomi, about two miles south-west of the site of Salamis itself. Yet the problem of the foundation-legend of Salamis as built after the Trojan War by Teucer,[20] son of Telamon, king of the Greek island of Salamis, could not be solved satisfactorily in terms of Late Bronze Age Enkomi. A number of classical Greek writers (*e.g.* Aeschylos and Pindar), mention Salamis specifically as the foundation of Teucer, and the name of Teucer is preserved down to the Roman period among the priestly and noble families of this city.[21] There are even indications that the Teucrian Salaminians (Sałamenski) were included among the Sea Peoples who were repulsed by Ramesses III in 1162 BC.[22]

Those who, like the present writer, place considerably confidence in mythological tradition, were however faced by the problem that we possessed no archaeological evidence from Salamis earlier than the eighth century BC. Though it was known that the Late Bronze Age town of Enkomi was destroyed and finally abandoned towards the middle of the eleventh century BC and was traditionally believed to have been succeeded by Salamis, this left a gap of three centuries which it was difficult to bridge. It was only in 1965 that the missing link was discovered, and mythological tradition once again proved true. A French expedition from the Institut F. Courby of the University of Lyon, headed by Professor J. Pouilloux, discovered remains at the south sector of Salamis that could be dated to the eleventh century BC.[23] On top of a hillock or ridge which extends along the northern side of the marshy land adjoining the harbour area, at about 100 metres from the seashore, a number of eleventh-century sherds came to light when trial trenches were dug down to the bed-rock. These sherds, of a local Cypriote fabric known as Proto-White Painted ware, may be dated to the first half of the eleventh century BC. It is as yet too early to determine the nature of the buildings with which this pottery is associated, and which existed along the crest of the hillocks that run east-west along the marshy land referred to above. Evidence for a mud-brick city-wall has been abundantly forthcoming during the last few seasons of excavations, and we will not be surprised if this wall proves to be of Late Bronze Age date. We know already how extensively mud-bricks were used during the Late Bronze Age at Enkomi and Kition for the construction of defensive walls. It was quite appropriate to build the city-wall along this strategic point of the ridge, thus forming the south-western extremity of the city's defences which dominated the harbour area.

During the same year, a chamber tomb dating to the first half of the eleventh century BC (contemporary with the ceramic material discovered on top of the ridge referred to above) was excavated roughly half a mile away to the west, about one hundred metres south of the site of the Roman 'temple of Zeus'. Topographically this discovery is of the utmost importance. If the early city of Salamis was built on the elevated ground immediately to the north of the marshy land adjoining the harbour area, then its necropolis extended to the west, with a perimeter about one mile from the sea-shore, though these distances are still to be determined precisely by more archaeological documentation. The pottery discovered in the tomb, as well as that from the stratigraphic trench on top of the ridge, points to the first half of the eleventh century, but we may legitimately suggest as an initial date for the foundation of Salamis a period several decades earlier, nearer 1100 BC. This date, as we know, is not far from that usually proposed for the 'return' of the heroes (*nostoi*) from the Trojan War and the expedition of Teucer and other Greeks to Cyprus. Here, therefore, we have archaeological evidence which substantiates most effectively the mythological tradition about the foundation of Salamis by Teucer.

Plates 1–3

We know that Enkomi was abandoned towards the middle of the eleventh century BC, as a result of a natural catastrophe (an earthquake or a flood),²⁴ and also perhaps after the silting up of its inner harbour; but this evacuation must have been gradual, and there was a time during the first half of the eleventh century when both Enkomi and Salamis coexisted, until the former completely yielded its place to the new harbour city by the sea-shore.

Salamis, from the earliest period of its existence, must have been an important city. To this the material found in the tomb referred to above (Salamis Tomb 1) bears eloquent witness: there were about 250 vases of a rich variety of form and decoration, gold jewellery (finger rings, ear-rings, pendants, rosettes and a needle), instruments of bronze and iron, and a scarab in faience. The style of the pottery throws much light on the cultural trends which existed in Cyprus during that period. Though the forms and decoration are basically Aegean (deriving from the Mycenaean 'Granary Style'), yet there are obvious Cretan elements, as for instance the use of pictorial motifs and composite triangles for the decoration, and at the same time Eastern (Phoenician) elements in various forms of vases and in the use of the Bichrome technique in the decoration. Side by side there are also traditional Cypriote elements, especially in the vase forms. Are we to associate this amalgamation of Western and Eastern elements in the style of pottery with the information which we have about Teucer, that he came to Cyprus together with ethnic elements from Anatolia and Phoenicia?²⁵

# The Age of Exuberance:
# The Necropolis in the Eighth and Seventh Centuries

We have already had a glimpse at the splendours of the initial stage of life at Salamis in the eleventh century BC. There is no way of telling why things changed during the subsequent centuries, but, as elsewhere in the island, here too we possess no archaeological evidence from these Dark Ages of Cypriote Archaeology, the tenth and ninth centuries BC. Our next encounter with Salamis, both in Archaeology and in History, is at the end of the eighth century. The Phoenicians, who started immigrating into Cyprus at least a century earlier, must have concentrated at Kition where their presence is lavishly illustrated by the recently discovered temple dating from about 800 BC. A new era begins for the whole of Cyprus towards the end of the eighth century, with the Assyrian domination over the island in 709 BC.[26]

King Sargon II boastfully records on a stele found at Kition how the kings of Cyprus, including the king of Salamis, submitted to him. We know, however, that the Assyrian rule over the island was a benevolent one; between 700 and 650 the Assyrian supremacy was confined to political and economic matters, and the Cypriote kingdoms were left free to develop their own culture. This benevolent rule developed into a kind of political independence during the years 650–570 BC which represents the most creative epoch of Cypriote civilization. Whilst the Phoenicians could not have had any political power in the island during the Assyrian supremacy, yet their influence in the cultural life of the island, though indirect, must have been considerable. The Cypriote kings, enjoying power and prosperity, were probably vying with each other in the display of luxury and wealth, and their monumental tombs show that they must have been regarded almost as divine creatures. In their palaces they must have introduced the mythical

*Salamis*

Plates 42,
IV–VIII

wealth of the Orient, obviously through the Phoenicians who are known to have been the carriers of the luxury goods of Western Asia, such as ivory furniture and exotic jewellery, to the royal courts of the Near East.[27] The kings were inevitably patrons of the arts, and it is not surprising that during the seventh century Cypriote arts and crafts reached an unprecedented degree of refined development. Though we know nothing about the royal palaces of this period, nor their exotic furniture, yet the objects found in tombs of the end of the eighth and the beginning of the seven century BC bear eloquent witness to the conditions just described. The few pieces of furniture accidentally discovered in the dromos of a looted tomb at Salamis have substantiated in the most convincing way the proverbial wealth and exuberant taste of the Cypriote kings, hitherto known only from the monumental architecture of their tombs.

But, whereas the window of Cyprus was wide open to the East, yet the island's Hellenic cultural roots were deep in its soil. This, as is well known, has been the pattern throughout the cultural history of Cyprus from the Late Bronze Age onwards; a confrontation, more often happy than hostile, between the Orient and the Occident. The end of the eighth century coincides with an important event in the Eastern Mediterranean, the establishment of colonies in the Near East by Greeks from the Cyclades, mainly from Eretria.[28] We may mention Al Mina in Syria and Tarsus in Cilicia. The presence of Cypriote influence in both of these groups of colonists, especially at Al Mina, is attested by the large amount of Cypriote pottery which these sites have produced. It has even been suggested that part of the population of Al Mina is likely to have been Cypriote, and that it might have been the Cypriots who led the Greeks to Al Mina. In any case, it is obvious that the Eretrians, on adventuring eastwards, must have stopped in Cyprus before embarking on the establishment of colonies on the opposite continent. Salamis, the easternmost Hellenic city in the Mediterranean must have been their main outpost. It is not surprising, therefore, that the recent excavations at Salamis produced quantities of Euboean pottery of the eighth century BC.[29] This new contact with the Aegean world must have revived the Hellenic consciousness of the Salaminians. It is quite natural, therefore, that this city should maintain the Hellenic tradition for several centuries afterwards, throughout the archaic period, and would become the champion of Hellenic ideals, especially during the classical period.

It is against this historical background that we should examine the recent discoveries in the eighth- and seventh-century 'royal' tombs of Salamis, not only for the intrinsic value of the material which they have produced but also for the information which they have yielded about political, social and cultural conditions in the island during the century following the Assyrian domination.

Tales of 'huge subterranean chambers' found in the plain of Salamis, between the forest and the Monastery of St Barnabas, were often narrated by villagers from Enkomi, the village which produced the most notorious of all the tomb looters in the district. These chambers were said to have been excavated 'long ago', and were often described as 'full of treasures of gold'; in a few cases more precise information could be obtained from old looters who were describing their own activities and discoveries. We know already of the excavations carried out by a British expedition in 1896, when one such 'subterranean chamber' was found under the large tumulus of earth which stands by itself in the plain of Salamis. That excavation, however, described in one single line in the excavation report, gave negative results.[30] In recent years the main preoccupation here of the Department of Antiquities of Cyprus was the excavation of the public buildings (Gymnasium and Theatre) within the city site of Salamis, and no attempt was made during the early stages of the new excavations which began in 1952 to extend this programme.

**Tomb 1:** In 1954 it was reported that a tomb had been discovered half-way between the Salamis forest and the Monastery of St Barnabas, at a short distance west of the large tumulus. Several attempts to loot this tomb (Tomb 1) were subsequently made, until in 1957 the Department of Antiquities, with Dr P. Dikaios in charge, undertook its excavation.[31] Though the chamber had been disturbed by looters, its lower layers remained intact. The tomb was built in a large trench extending from east to west cut into the natural clayey rock. It took the form of a rectangular chamber measuring 4.70m. × 5m. and 2m. in height, the western part built of boulders. The side walls curved inwards and were covered with plaster and the roof consisted of long slabs of schist. The chamber had a monumental façade, built of well-dressed blocks of soft white limestone, 9.45m. wide. In the middle, in front of the stomion, there was a recess serving as a kind of propylaeum, 4.60m. wide and 1m. deep, with two rectangular pillars on either side. The top of the façade was decorated with a cornice of which only fragments were found. The dromos, cut in the clayey rock, had a sloping floor, and its sides narrowed towards the entrance to 5.20m. There were two burials from different periods in the chamber, but only the lower (earlier) survived in more than fragmentary condition. It consisted of a bronze cauldron, buried in a pit in the floor, containing the cremated remains of the dead wrapped in a cloth, in true 'Homeric' fashion.[32] In fact traces of a pyre were found on the floor of the dromos, on which the corpse was burnt. This is a burial-custom which must have been introduced to Cyprus by newcomers from Greece and may well be connected, as we shall see below, with the arrival of Euboean Greeks in the island during their journeys eastward. Amongst the ashes inside the cauldron were a necklace of gold and rock-crystal beads and several thin sheets of gold; similar sheets of gold, in the shape of small discs, were also found on the pyre in the dromos, and it is obvious that they belonged to the garments of the deceased. Here we have, therefore, a tomb where a Cypriote noble lady or a princess was buried in the middle of the eighth century BC, to judge by the pottery discovered inside the chamber and in the dromos. This included a quantity of Greek Geometric pottery (twenty-seven pots in all), comprising bowls and skyphoi, as well as a crater. There is a tendency among scholars who have studied these vases recently to identify them as of Euboean origin. If this identification is correct, then it could tie up perfectly with the new burial-custom of cremation, and with the Euboean colonists stopping at Salamis en route for the East referred to earlier in this chapter. The second

*The Age of Exuberance*

(disturbed) burial was an inhumation and may be dated to the end of the early seventh century BC.

Two burial-layers were distinguished in the filling of the dromos, each associated with the two burials in the chamber. Each contained large amphorae, both plain and painted. The skeletons of two horses were found on the floor of the dromos, associated with traces of the wooden parts of a chariot. These, however, were very much disturbed when part of the filling of the tomb was removed to uncover the stomion of the chamber for the second burial. Four horses and traces of a two-poled chariot were found in association with the second burial. The wooden parts of the chariot had decayed completely, but had left their impressions in the soil; some of the metal parts, for example the bronze rings on the yoke, were however preserved *in situ*. The metal parts of the horses' gear – blinkers and head bands of bronze and bits of iron, were also found *in situ*. This, then, is Tomb 1 in the necropolis of Salamis. Its discovery is of outstanding importance because it taught the future excavator of the necropolis what to expect in the dromoi of other built 'royal' tombs which were to be excavated in the same region.

Plate 6

Plate 8

It is now obvious, but *post eventum*, that similar phenomena (horse burials) occurred also in the dromos of at least one tomb at Tamassos, but at the time of the excavation (1888) only items of the bronze gear of the horses were collected and these were thought by the excavator to belong to armour. The custom of horse burial must have been widespread in the island, and apart from Salamis we have now found it as far away as Palaepaphos on the south-west coast of the island.[33]

The excavation of Tomb 1 immediately brought to mind 'Homeric' burial customs. The cremation of the dead, the collection of the bones which were wrapped in cloth and placed in a cauldron, the large amphorae in the dromos which must have contained 'olive oil or honey' and finally the sacrifice of the horses in honour of the dead, all recall the well-known description in the *Iliad* of the burial of Patroklos.[34] It soon became evident that an important field of research lay ahead. A more systematic excava-

SECTION A-A'

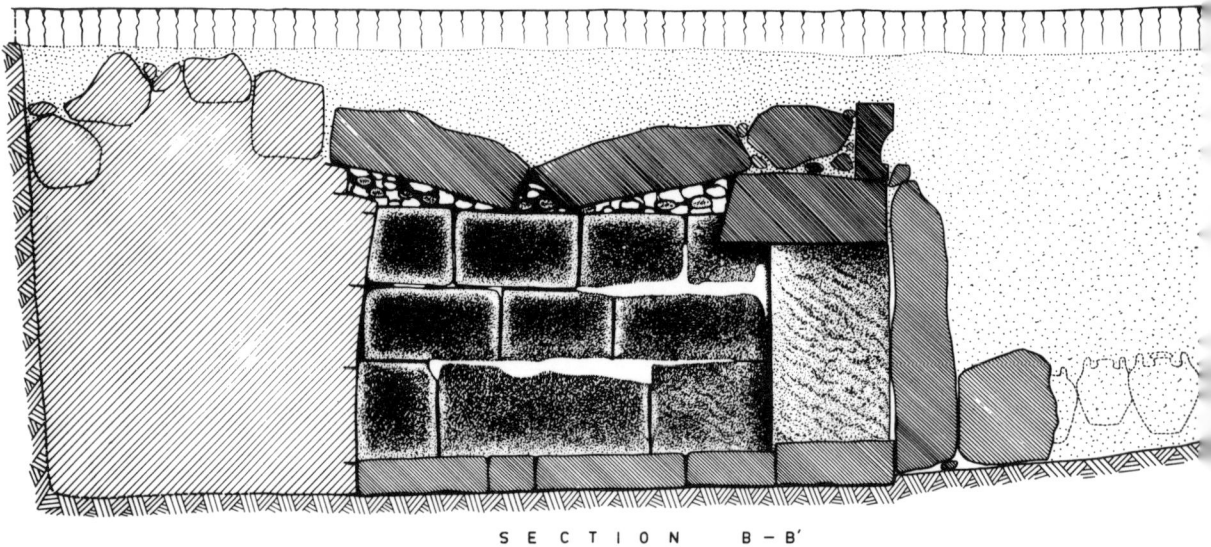

SECTION B-B'

tion of the necropolis seemed necessary, and this highly rewarding task was undertaken by the present writer for the Department of Antiquities of the Republic of Cyprus.

**Tomb 2** was excavated in 1962, following information supplied by the man who entered it some fifty years ago.[35] The general architectural layout of this tomb was similar to that of Tomb 1, but its façade was flat, with no recess at the stomion. The cornice

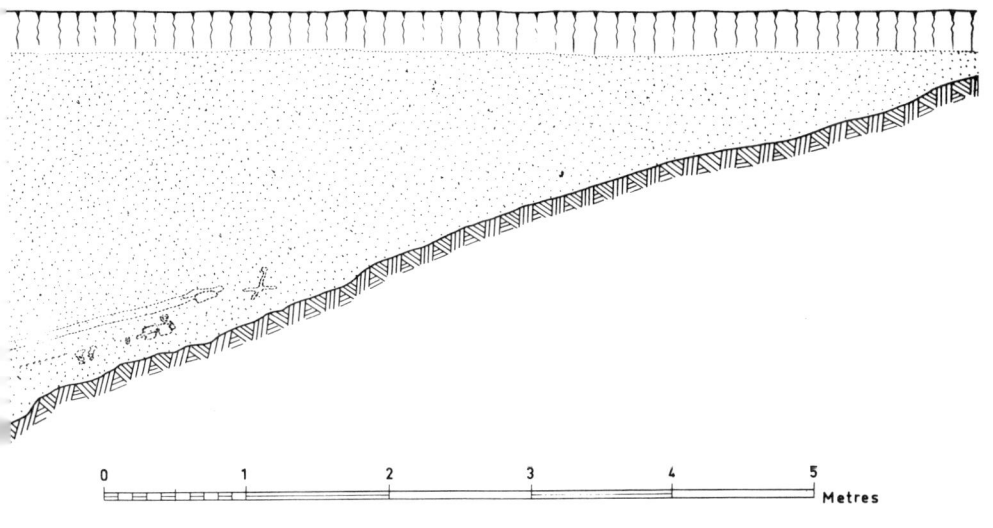

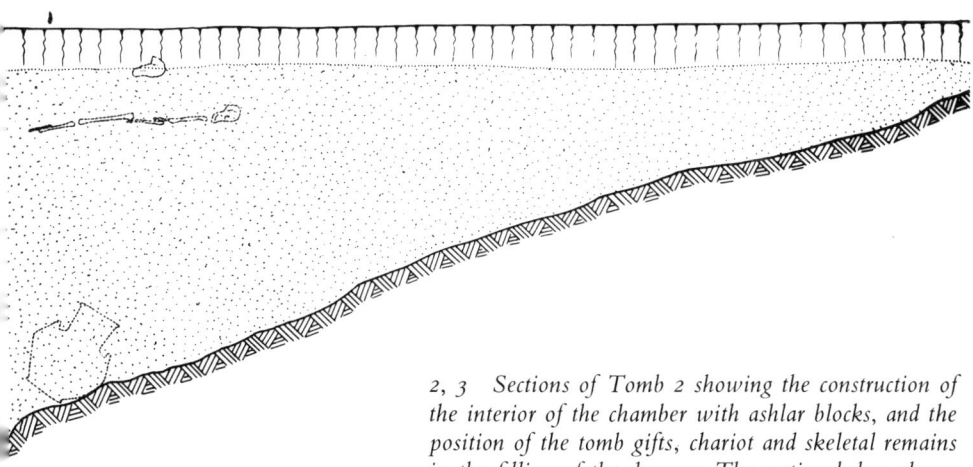

2, 3 Sections of Tomb 2 showing the construction of the interior of the chamber with ashlar blocks, and the position of the tomb gifts, chariot and skeletal remains in the filling of the dromos. The section below shows also the position of the skeleton of the sacrificed slave

along the top of the façade, made of carved blocks of white limestone, was found in perfect condition. The carving is in the same style as that of the cornice of Tomb 1, consisting of a wide cavetto between two fillets, the upper fillet slightly projecting beyond the lower. The chamber is rectangular, measuring 3.10m. × 2.20m., with walls curving inwards; the height from the paved floor to the flat roof is 1.85m. A large rectangular slab of hard limestone

*Salamis*

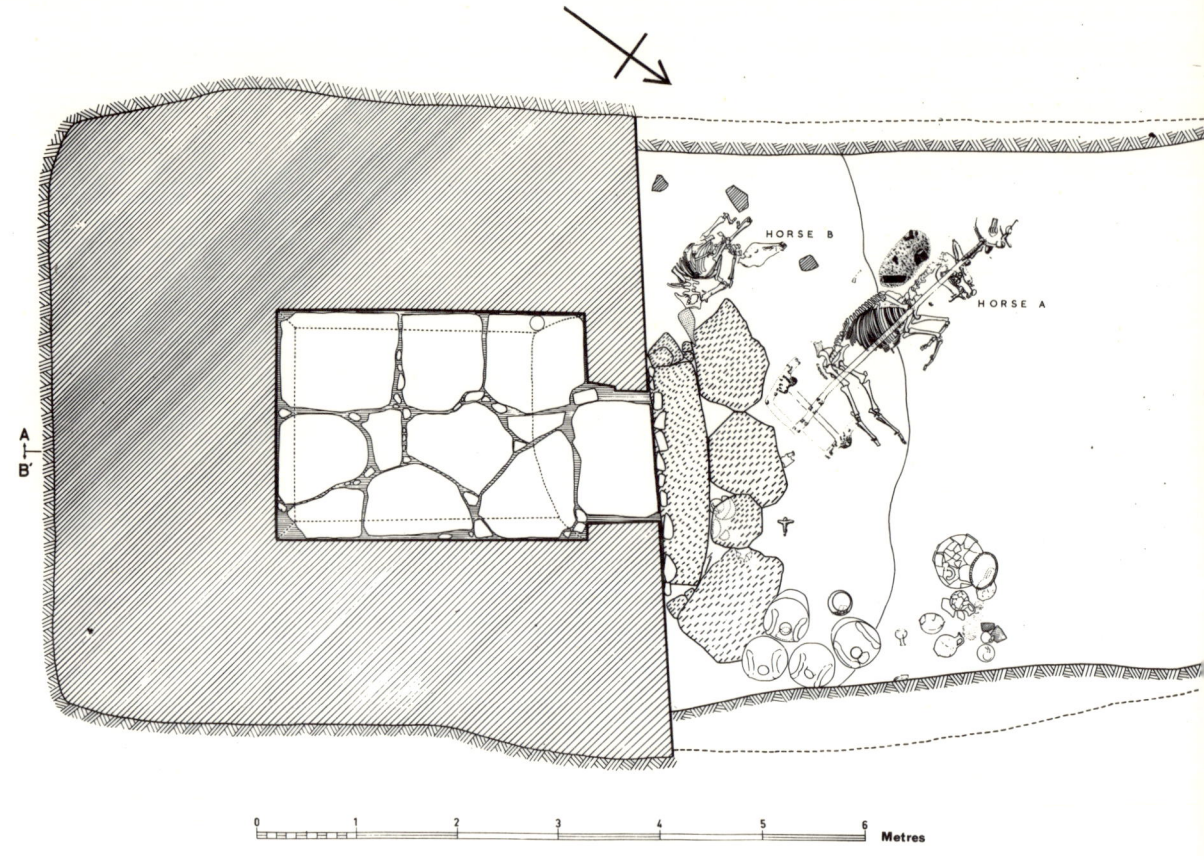

4  Plan of Tomb 2 showing the floor of the chamber and the floor of the spacious dromos in front of it, with the hearse and the skeletal remains of the two asses in situ. The amphorae and other vases are on the left-hand side of the dromos

*Figs 2, 3*

was found *in situ* blocking the entrance to the tomb, but the looters had entered it by breaking a slab of the roof. The sloping dromos was 9.25m. long; its width at the façade of the chamber was 6.10m. and it narrowed to 4.50m. near the entrance.

With the utmost care we excavated the soil filling of the dromos. About 60cm. from the surface of the cultivated soil, and about 40cm. from the top of the original filling of the dromos a human skeleton was found near the western side, about 2.50m. from the

*The Age of Exuberance*

façade of the chamber. It was lying flat, buried in the homogeneous filling of the dromos and as there was no trace whatsoever of a pit, it was quite obvious that the corpse was buried at the time when the dromos was filled up with soil. The hands were joined as if fastened together in front of the body, and the legs were close together. Other skeletal remains were found nearer to the surface in the filling of the dromos and were evidently disturbed by the plough. We believe that these human skeletons are those of servants buried at the same time as their master, having been killed to serve him in the after-life. This custom is already known from elsewhere in Cyprus: from Lapithos (early first millennium BC), from Tamassos (archaic period) and from Vouni Palace (classical period). Slave-burials were known in Mycenaean Greece, and Homer was familiar with this practice when he described the sacrifice of nine young Trojans on the pyre of Patroklos. Similar customs were also practised in Scythia, in association with horse burials.[36]

On the floor of the dromos, and near the entrance to the chamber, the skeleton of a quadruped was found, lying in a natural position; above the animal's body were the traces of a wooden pole which had left its impression in the soil – clearly the pole of the vehicle associated with this animal. The animal's gear (bronze blinkers, a bronze head band), all decorated in repoussé with stylized lotus flowers, and the iron bits, were found *in situ* on its head. The second animal was sought next to the first one, but no traces of it were found there, only its gear, lying on the floor at a short distance from the head of the first animal. Then, in the corner which is formed by the façade of the chamber and the western side wall of the dromos the skeleton of the other quadruped was found, with its neck vertical, head horizontal, forelegs in an upright position, and with the body slightly raised from the ground and supported on the hind legs. All round it on the floor were lumps of stone rubble. We soon realized that here was the second member of the yoked team who, having seen its companion put to death, must have freed itself from the harness, and fled to the corner, while from above stones were thrown at it and the funeral attendants

Plate 9
*Fig. 4*

Plate 11

Plate 12

Plate 10

poured down earth upon it. It was in an effort to escape that this animal had been buried alive in the dromos. An expert examination of the skeletal remains of both quadrupeds showed that they were a pair of asses (not horses). This is important, considering that in the larger 'royal' tombs in the same necropolis, as we shall see below, horses were sacrificed, not asses.

The vehicle which was drawn by the two asses was a hearse without a 'box', having a flat 'floor' carried on two wheels. The metal parts of the vehicle, all of iron, had survived *in situ*, as for instance the thick bearing 'shoes' inside the Π-shaped slot below the 'floor' and on either side of it, in which the axle revolved; there were also various nails which had fastened the wooden parts together. Although all the wood had rotted away, careful observation and measurement still made it possible to reconstruct the entire hearse. Clay models of such vehicles are known from the archaic period in Cyprus. The main part of the vehicle could easily be detached from the pole for burial inside the chamber. Similar carts were used in Greece – we see them depicted on archaic and classical Greek vases, in association with weddings and funerals.[37] The ancestor of the Cypriote hearse, however, must have had a Near Eastern origin.

On the floor of the dromos, mainly against its eastern wall, lay a row of large clay amphorae, as well as dishes, jugs and clay lamps. The amphorae, which had earthen lids, were empty, except for a spongy substance in the bottom, obviously the remnants of their organic contents – olive oil or possibly honey, if we may draw an analogy from the Homeric description of the burial of Patroklos referred to above. The jugs were all covered with a dark greyish substance which on analysis proved to be a plating of tin applied to their surface in order to give them a metallic appearance. It must be remembered how much bronze and silver jugs were appreciated in Homeric times. Such metal vases are usually regarded as Phoenician; they found their way to many centres throughout the Mediterranean, as far as Italy and Spain. The same custom of plating the surface of clay vessels with tin was observed recently on Mycenaean vases from the Athenian Agora. At Salamis, as we

1 A jug of Bichrome I ware found by a French Expedition in an eleventh century BC tomb at the South Sector of Salamis (Tomb I, 144). The globular body is decorated with five groups of concentric circles containing bichrome rosettes

2 A vase of Proto-White Painted ware, in the form of a bird, found in the same tomb as the jug in Plate 1, above. (Tomb I, 127). The sides of the body are decorated with friezes of latticed lozenges; the wings, eyes and other details of the body are plastically rendered

3 Detail from the decoration of a kalathos of White Painted I ware, found in the same tomb as the pottery in Plates 1–2. It shows a wild goat within a rectangular panel; this motif is of Cretan origin and must have been borrowed from Subminoan vase-painting, a phenomenon which is quite common in Cyprus in the eleventh century BC, both in vase-painting and in other arts and crafts

4 A necklace consisting of six gold ribbed beads, five cylindrical links of gold and six globular beads of rock-crystal, found in Tomb 1 of the Royal Necropolis of Salamis. It must have belonged to a 'princess' whose incinerated skeletal remains were found together with the necklace in a deep bronze bowl wrapped in a cloth, in a true 'Homeric' fashion (cf. Iliad XXIV, 796). Eighth century BC

5 A Greek imported crater of Middle Geometric type, found in the same tomb as the necklace of Plate 4. This tomb produced a large quantity of Greek geometric pottery, mainly skyphoi and shallow bowls, dating to the second quarter of the eighth century BC. Their provenance may be either Attica or Euboea, and their presence in a tomb at Salamis may be indicative of the role which this city played during the eastward expansion of the Greek colonists during the eighth and seventh centuries BC. Craters of this form have also been found in other parts of Cyprus, and were occasionally imitated by local artists both in shape and decoration

6–8 The dromos of Tomb 1 in the Royal Necropolis of Salamis. *Above*, large amphorae piled against the façade of the chamber and the sides of the dromos. *Below, left*, the built chamber, with its façade of ashlar blocks of limestone; a huge slab seals the entrance. *Below, right*, traces left in the soil by the wood of the two-poled chariot which was buried in the dromos; the solid wheels and the yoke also left their impressions on the floor of the dromos

9–10 The dromos of Tomb 2 in the Royal Necropolis of Salamis where a hearse driven by two asses was dedicated. One of the animals and traces of the hearse are seen *above* and *below* is one of the asses who tried to escape and was buried alive. The animal is here seen with its neck vertical, its head in a horizontal position, the forelegs are bent in an effort to lift his body up. His bronze gear can be seen *in situ*, *above*, next to the first horse

11–12 The heads of the asses sacrificed in the dromos of Tomb 9 were decorated with blinkers and head bands of bronze. Plate 12 shows these in position on the head of one of the asses *(below, left)*; those of the second ass who tried to free himself are seen nearby *(above, right)*. The two pairs of blinkers consisted of one plain piece (19.5 cm. long) and another, decorated in repoussé, with three lotus buds (17.5 cm. long). The head bands, which consisted of two hinged pieces (46 cm. long) were decorated in *repoussé* with lotus and papyrus flowers; they terminated in an anthemium. The iron bits were also found, and Plate 12 shows one of the asses with the bit in his mouth

13, 14 *Above*, a pair of ivory blinkers found in the dromos of Tomb 47, in association with the horses of the second burial. They are decorated with three buds of flowers, in the fashion of the metallic blinkers of Tomb 1 (*cf.* Plate 11). Homer refers to ivory blinkers in the *Iliad* IV, 141–142; they are also referred to in the Linear B tablets from Knossos. The head bands of the horses of the second burial were of bronze, *right*, and decorated with embossed and cut-out papyrus flowers, lotus flowers and anthemia

15 The same tomb produced, among the offerings found in the dromos, an Egyptian scarab of paste, *left*, of the reign of Osorkon I (926–881 BC); this obviously must have been an heirloom, as Tomb 47 dates to the eighth–seventh centuries BC

16–18 The large and monumental Tomb 47, *opposite*, was used twice, first at the end of the eighth century, and a second time at the beginning of the seventh. Two horses driving a vehicle were sacrificed on the cemented floor of the dromos during the first burial, *opposite, below*. One of them is lying flat in a natural position, but the second one who tried to escape twisted and broke his neck round the yoke; his head was found lying on his ribs. Both horses had blinkers and head bands of a perishable material (leather ?) covered with thin sheets of gold which were found *in situ*. The hearse on which the corpse was carried to the tomb must have been detachable from the pole and was buried in the chamber. The horses remained yoked, and the wood of their yoke and pole left their impressions in the soil. During the second burial a large trench was dug into the filling of the dromos in order to gain access to the entrance to the chamber. Six horses were sacrificed in honour of the dead during this burial: four of them were driving a quadriga and two a biga, *below*, all found lying about one metre above the level of the floor of the dromos. The second burial did not disturb the skeletons of horses of the first burial (Plate 17) the front bands and blinkers of which were of ivory (Plate 13) and of bronze (Plate 14).

The chamber of this tomb was destroyed by stone-robbers, who also removed the stone which dressed the sides of the dromos, but the monumental staircase in front of the propyleum remained intact (Plate 17). The architectural style of this tomb was the key to the identification of the so-called Tomb of St Catherine (Plates 19–22)

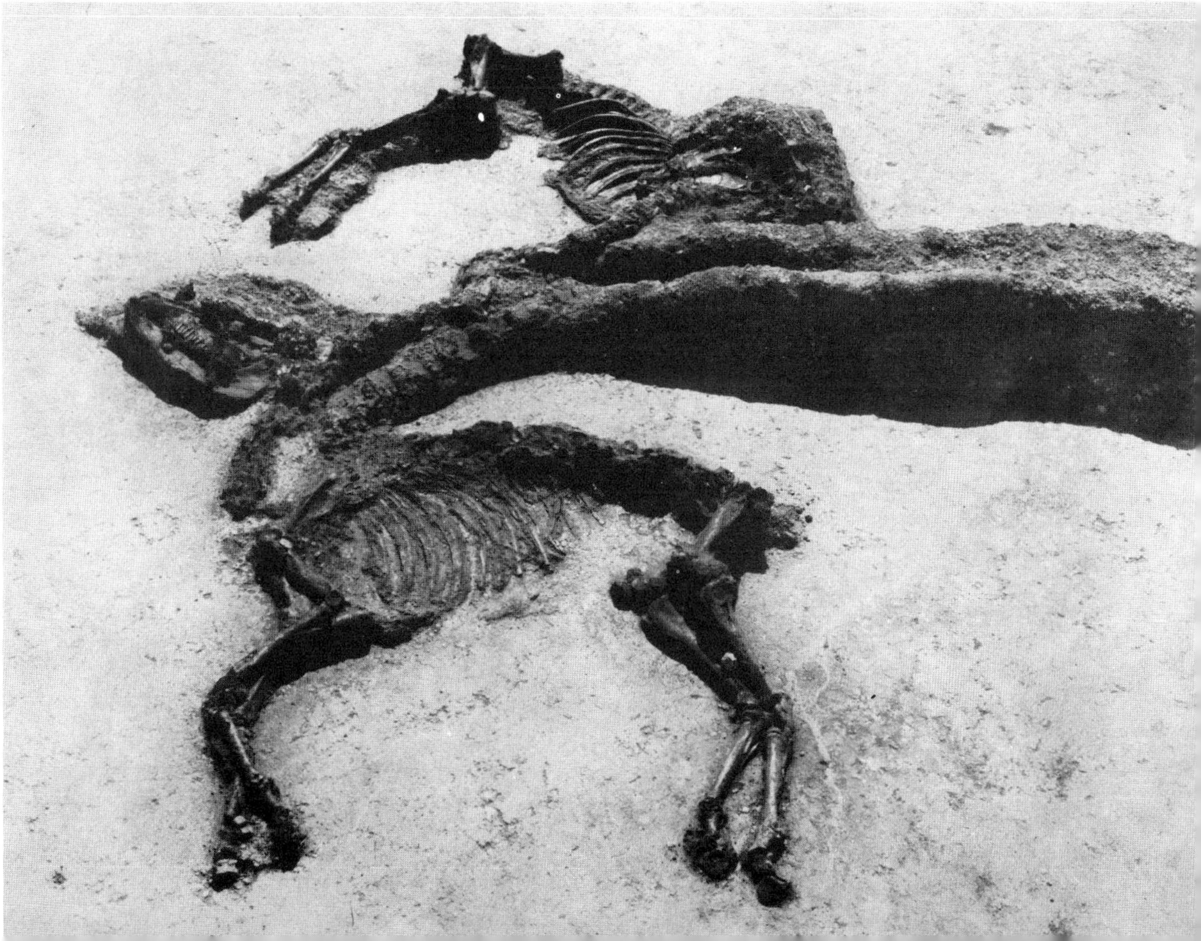

19–22 Tomb 50, previously known as the Tomb or Prison of St Catherine, was an architectural riddle for a whole century to students of Cypriote archaeology. Its vaulted chamber, *above*, visible already in the Middle Ages, was described as a 'Graeco-Roman' tomb by modern scholars, who failed to recognize the two periods in its construction. Originally there was a built tomb with a chamber, a propyleum with a corniced façade (Plate 20), and a large dromos in front, as Tomb 47 (Plate 17). It was in the Roman period that the area of the propyleum was turned into a rectangular vaulted chamber. Excavation revealed a large dromos to the east of the vaulted chamber where two skeletons of horses were found, and enough material to date the original tomb to the seventh century BC

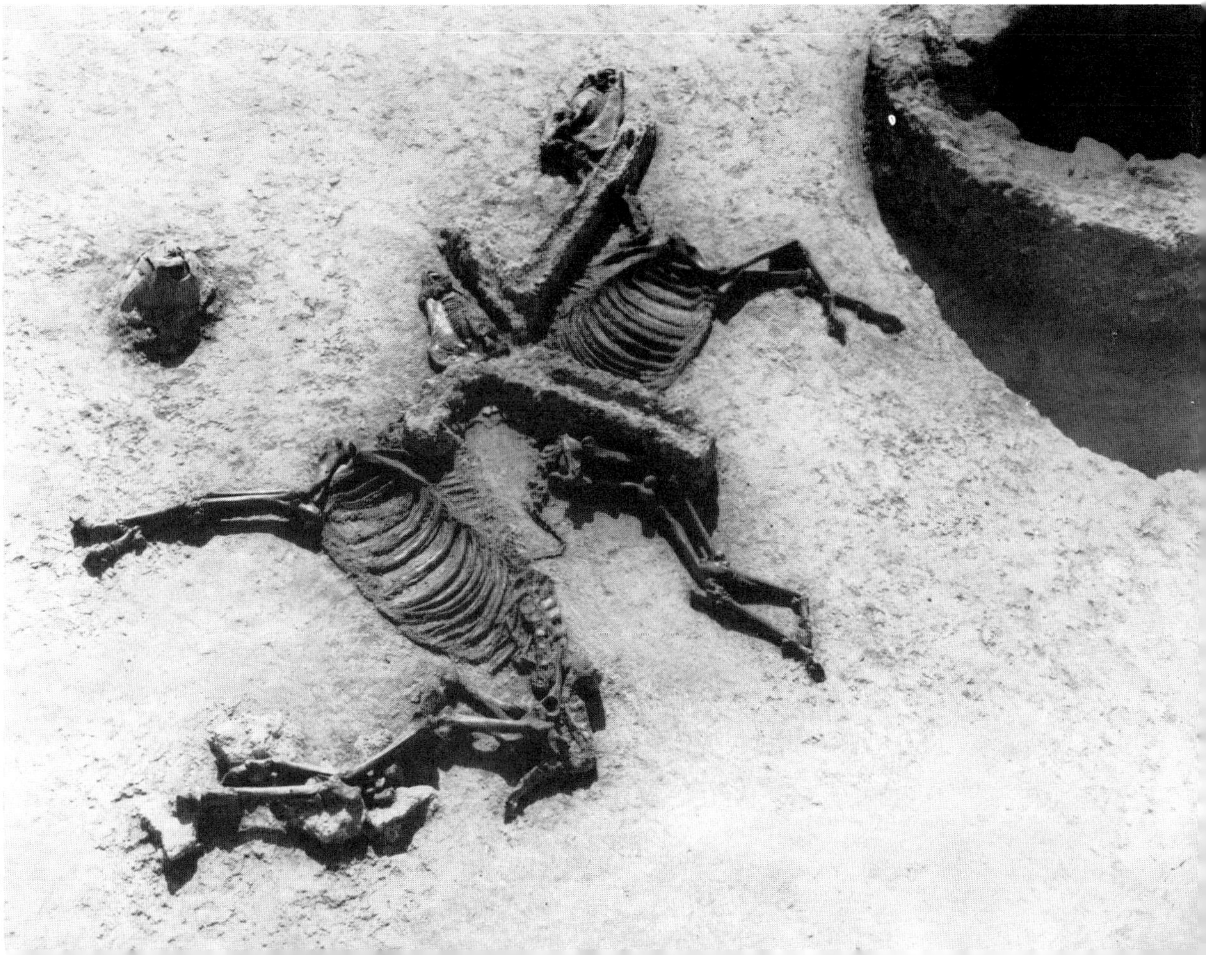

23, 24 A large monumental built tomb was found under the tumulus of earth which dominates the plain of Salamis: Tomb 3, looted by the villagers in the nineteenth century and excavated by British archaeologists in 1896. Its architecture shows the obvious influence of Asia Minor, where a number of built tombs under tumuli have come to light. In the filling of the dromos of Tomb 3 large numbers of vases were found, including an amphora bearing a painted syllabic inscription below one of the handles (Plate 24), which reads in Greek 'of olive oil' = 'an amphora of olive oil'. This is another 'Homeric' element in the burial customs of Salamis, recalling the offering of jars of olive oil in the funeral of Patroklos (cf. the Iliad XXIII, 71–72)

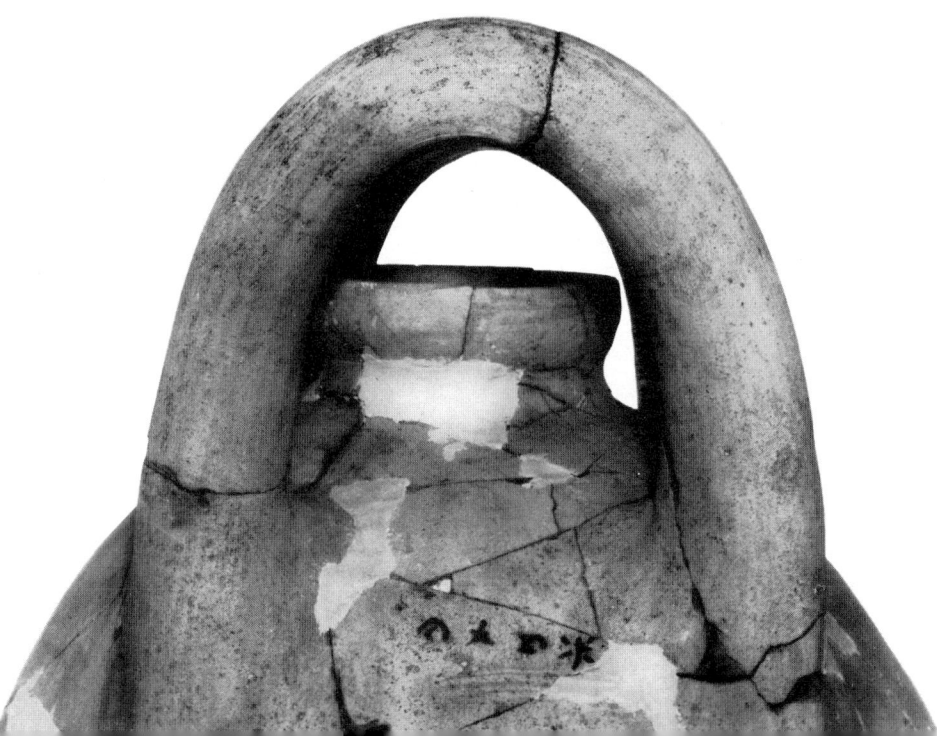

25, 26 Traces of two chariots were found in the dromos of Tomb 3. In one of them a silver-studded sword of iron was found, *left*, still preserving traces of the wood and leather of its sheath. Homer often refers to such silver-studded swords. The yoke of one of the two chariots was decorated with four standards of bronze, in the shape of nine-petalled flowers, *above*, whose purpose was obviously ornamental. End of the seventh century BC

27–30 Tomb 31 (Plate 30) is one of the smallest built tombs in the Royal Necropolis, but one of the rare ones which had their burial chamber intact. On the floor of the chamber, lying in a pit, an amphora was found containing the incinerated remains of the dead, *below*. In another pit on the floor of the chamber a large number of diadems of thin gold sheets were found; some of them are decorated in repoussé with chariot scenes, *above* (length 9 cm.), or with sphinxes, others are plain. On the floor of the dromos the skeletons of two unyoked asses were found, symmetrically arranged, but with no gear on their heads. This was obviously the tomb of a nobleman of an intermediate class, not to be compared with those of the previously described tombs. Tomb 31 dates to the seventh century BC

31, 32 Large numbers of vases, some of unusual shape, were found in the intact burial chamber of Tomb 31 (*see also* Plates 27–30). *Above*, is an example shaped like a feeding bottle and *below*, a lug-handled jar standing on three looped legs

shall see, it was extensively practised.[38] The pottery from the floor of the dromos dates to the end of the Cypro-Archaic I period, *i.e.* towards the end of the seventh century BC. There was, however, an earlier burial in about 700 BC. In the filling of the dromos was found pottery from the end of the Cypro-Archaic III period, as well as fragments of skeletal remains of quadrupeds and the metal fittings of a vehicle. These must have belonged to an earlier horse and chariot burial, disturbed at the time of the second burial when the filling of the dromos was taken out in order to make room for the latter. Naturally, when the dromos was filled up again, these scanty remains from the first burial were replaced in the fill above the second.

The inside of the chamber was thoroughly disturbed. Fragments of a human skull were found, but it cannot be ascertained to which burial (first or second) they belonged. Nor is it possible to determine whether both burials were inhumations or whether one was a cremation. Apart from the pottery found broken and mixed with the soil inside the chamber, having obviously been considered by the looters not worth taking, we found a remarkable silver bowl lying in a small shallow pit in the floor. It measured 3.8cm. in height and 14.5cm. in diameter. When found its surface was completely corroded, and it was sent to the laboratory of the Institute of Archaeology of the University of London for treatment. On cleaning, the inside surface was seen to have been finely engraved; careful examination and detailed photography brought to light a twofold decoration: when the initial design had become worn, a completely different pattern was evidently re-engraved upon it.

The decoration of the first period consists of an Egyptianizing composition of human figures in a central medallion, and four narrow zones encircling the inside of the bowl; three of them are filled with stylized floral motifs, while the fourth contains non-sensical Egyptian hieroglyphs. The later decoration consists of a central medallion containing a winged sphinx and three encircling zones of which the outer is ornamented with panels filled alternately with stylized floral motifs and winged sphinxes; the other two zones contain abstract linear motifs. A series of such bowls exist, most of which have been found in Cyprus. They are usually considered to be Phoenician, though one cannot exclude the possibility that they might have been made by Cypriots under strong Phoenician influence. We know that such vessels of silver were carried to the various markets of the Mediterranean by Phoenician merchants and that Homer admired them as 'works of the Sidonians'.[39]

Though the material found in Tombs 1 and 2 was of considerable importance, and the burial-customs in each case were highly significant, yet their architecture was not as monumental as that of some of the tombs which will be described below.

It was in 1964 that the present writer, as Director of the Department of Antiquities, planned the systematic excavation of the necropolis of Salamis. At a distance of about 50m. east of Tomb 2 a block of stone visible above the cultivated surface of a field indicated the probable existence of a built tomb. And so it proved. **Tomb 47** is one of the largest in the cemetery, with a spacious cemented dromos leading to a monumental propylaeum in front of a chamber built of enormous blocks of well dressed stone. However, not only was the chamber found looted, but much of its stone had been robbed. Old villagers of Enkomi still clearly recalled how some fifty or more years ago looters from Idalion robbed the tomb, using dynamite to break through its monolithic roof.[40]

The dromos of the tomb, facing the city to the east, measured 20m. in length, 13.65m. in maximum width (near the façade) diminishing to 10.50m. near the entrance. It sloped down to a flight of four steps of good masonry which gave access to a paved propylaeum, measuring 10.65m. × 4.60m. The propylaeum has the shape of the Greek letter Π and behind it lies the rectangular chamber of the tomb, measuring 4.00m. × 2.20m. The monolithic slab which formed the saddle roof had been robbed together with the large blocks of the façade of the chamber. At the top of the façade there was a cornice in the same style as those of Tombs 1 and 2, but only a fragment of it survived; it was found in the looters' pits in

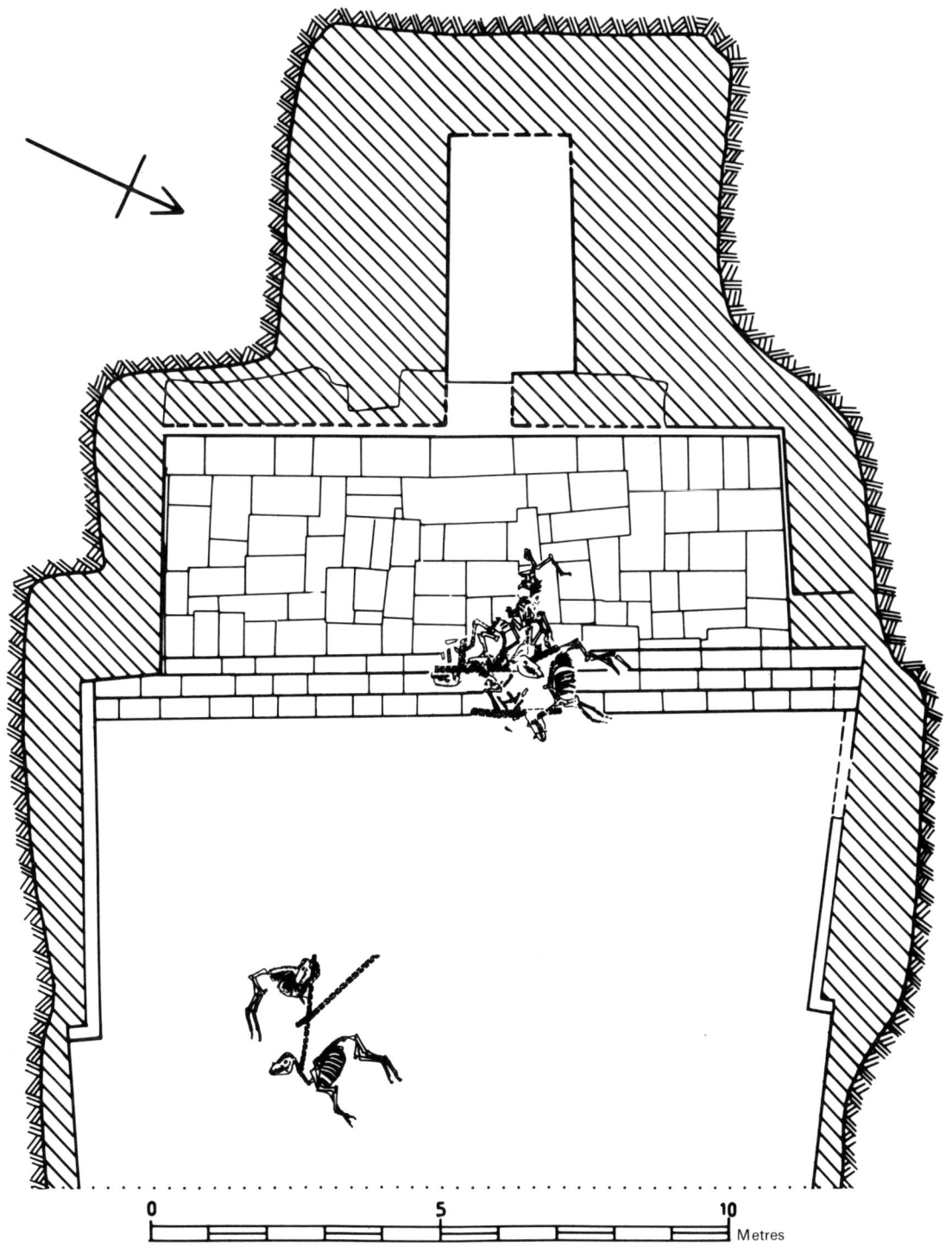

5 *Plan of Tomb 47 showing in detail its propylaeum and spacious dromos; near the steps of the propylaeum are shown the skeletal remains of the six horses of the second burial period; the skeletons of the two horses of the first period are shown on the floor of the dromos*

*Salamis*

the dromos. This fragment, however, led us to identify the nearby 'Tomb of St Catherine', which is of exactly the same architectural type and which will be discussed below (p. 55).

Inside the chamber nothing was found apart from some of the stone-robbers' tools. Most of the filling of the dromos, however, remained intact, and this produced, as usual, interesting results.

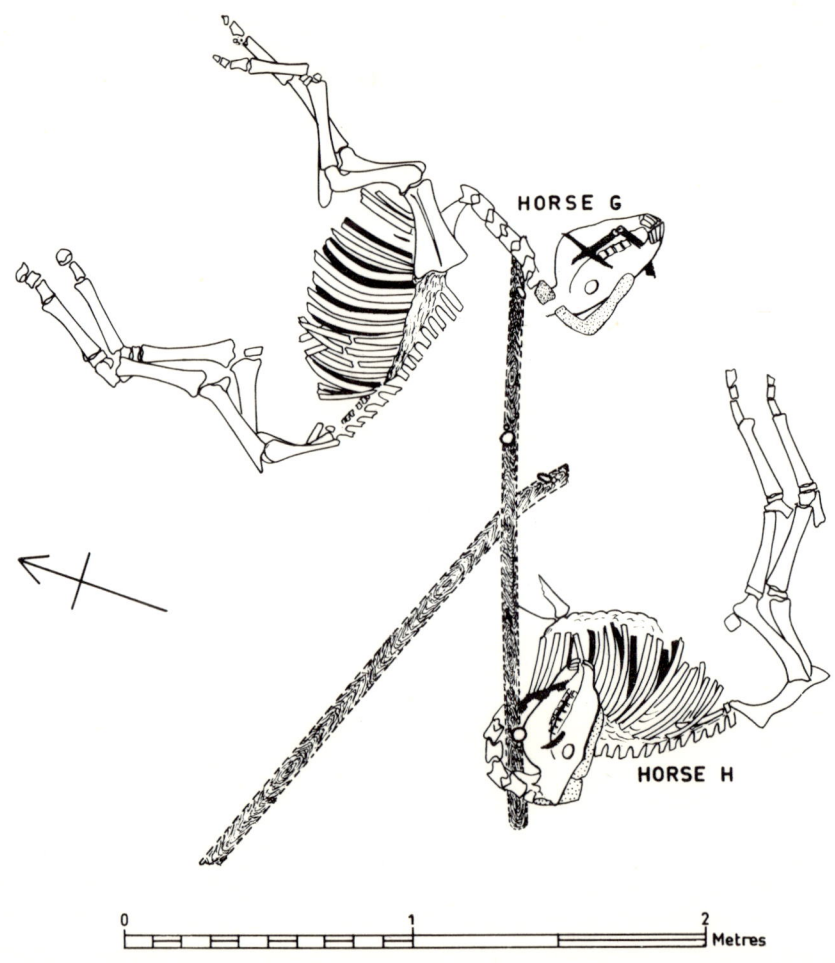

*6 The skeletal remains of the two horses of the first burial period on the floor of the dromos of Tomb 47. The wood of the pole and the yoke left their impressions in the soil; the chariot box itself, which was detachable, must have been buried with the deceased inside the chamber*

The burials in the dromos, and consequently in the chamber, may be reconstructed as follows: There was a first burial towards the end of the eighth century BC, when the tomb was built. The corpse was brought from the city on a hearse, the platform of which was detachable from the pole, and was buried in the chamber; the two horses, still yoked and with the pole of the hearse attached to the yoke, were sacrificed in front of the steps of the propylaeum. The first horse was killed and fell in a natural position on the floor, but its fellow, as in the case of Tomb 2, in attempting to run away, twisted its neck round the yoke and broke it in falling; its head remained lying on its ribs. Both horses had their gear *in situ*: it included iron bits, blinkers and the head bands of thin sheets of gold which must have been attached to pieces of some perishable material (leather?).

This burial is well dated by four large White Painted III ware amphorae of the end of the eighth century BC. These were not disturbed during the second burial period as they had been placed on either side of the dromos, lying against the built side walls. They obviously contained liquids, as did almost all those in the built tombs of this necropolis.

The same tomb was used for a second burial during the first half of the seventh century. In order to gain access to the stomion of the chamber a ditch was dug into the soil filling of the dromos about a metre above the original floor level. The hearse bearing the deceased was drawn by the horses through this ditch near the stomion for burial inside the chamber, and then the horses were sacrificed. Six skeletons of horses were found, four for a quadriga and two for a biga. They were all yoked and the poles were attached to the yoke. It is not certain whether one or two corpses were buried at the same time. The fact that two different vehicles each capable of being detached from their poles were used makes the latter seem more likely. What is certain, from the stratification of the filling of the dromos, is that all six horses were sacrificed simultaneously, and not on two different occasions. There must have been a scene of great confusion when the horses were killed one after the other. As usual, the first horse fell and lay in a natural

*Salamis*

Plates 13, 14

position, but the others were found in positions which betrayed the struggle to free themselves from the yoke. The horses had their gear *in situ*; the blinkers and head bands of two of the horses were of ivory[41] carved with lotus flowers and anthemia; the rest were of bronze, all decorated in repoussé with anthemia and stylized lotus flowers.

Plate IX

Pottery belonging to this second burial was found in abundance. Of particular interest was a stand with a long stem consisting of two nude female figures standing back to back; they are painted in red, black and white. A number of juglets had tin plating on their surface, as in the case of those from Tomb 2. In the filling of the dromos, and clearly belonging to the first burial, there was an Egyptian scarab of paste with the cartouche of Osorkon I, second king of the XXII Dynasty (926–881 BC), obviously an heirloom. There was also a gold-plated fibula.

Plate 15

Half-way between the western limit of the Salamis Forest and the Monastery of St Barnabas, about 90m. north-east of Tomb 47, lies a megalithic monument which is known as the **'Tomb'**, or **'Prison of St Catherine'**. To this day it is used as a chapel, dedicated to St Catherine. The excavators of 1965 found a large vaulted chamber half-buried in the gound, with an entrance and a small staircase to the east. On the west it communicated with a small rectangular chamber, which was used as a holy of holies by the priest and in the centre of which a crudely shaped altar was erected. The larger vaulted chamber housed the ikon of St Catherine, a few offerings and furniture. This monument impressed medieval travellers and visitors to Salamis more than any other in the area of the city,[42] and already in the fourteenth century a German traveller referred to it in his memoirs as the 'Chapel of St Catherine'. The large size of its stones impressed scholars of the nineteenth century, and Ohnefalsch-Richter described it in a special study entitled *A Prehistoric Building at Salamis*, as 'one of the most interesting of its kind in Cyprus and the East'. He made several suggestions regarding its identification: 'a spring or well-house, a temple or sanctuary, perhaps a tomb, a treasure house or a place of refuge in time of trouble'. A small excavation round it was

Plate 19

Plate 20

*The Age of Exuberance*

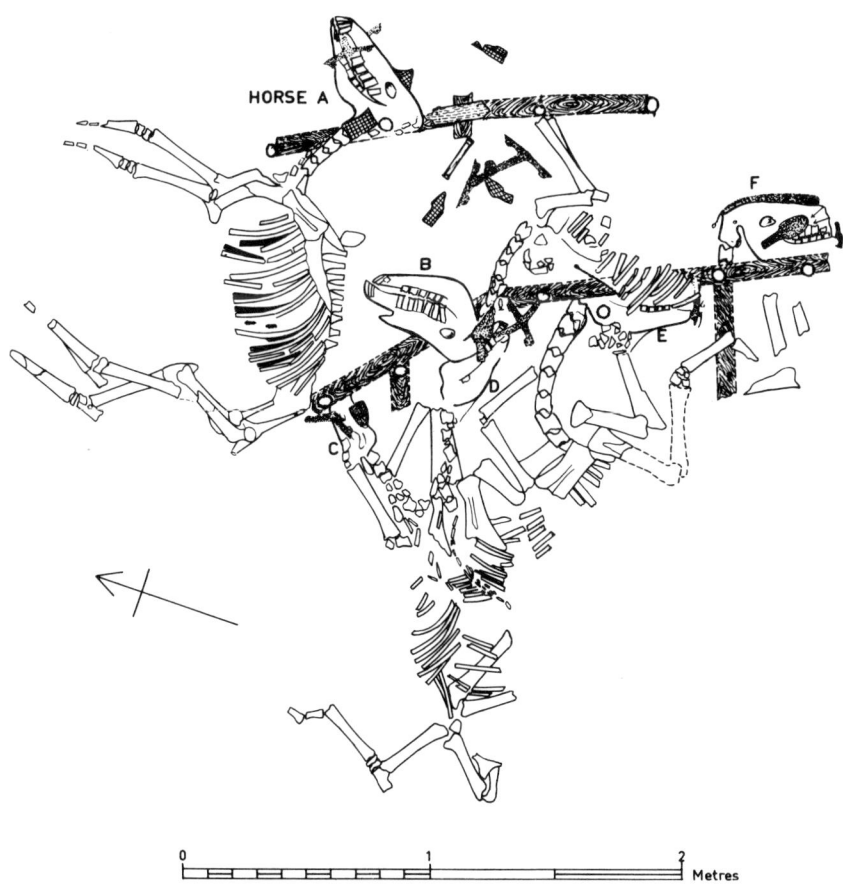

7  The skeletal remains of the six horses of the second burial period in Tomb 47. Traces of the wood of the poles and yokes of the two vehicles were left in the soil, within the filling of the dromos, about one metre above its floor

undertaken in 1914 by Sir John Myres, and two papers on this monument were read at the Society of Antiquaries of London in the same year by Myers and Jeffery (Inspector of the Monuments of Cyprus).[43] They concluded that it was a Graeco-Roman tomb and this has been the prevailing opinion since then.

We have already mentioned that a fragment of a large stone cornice found in the dromos of Tomb 47 led us immediately to compare it with similar cornices round the inside of the vaulted chamber of the Tomb of St Catherine. This was a real 'key' to the

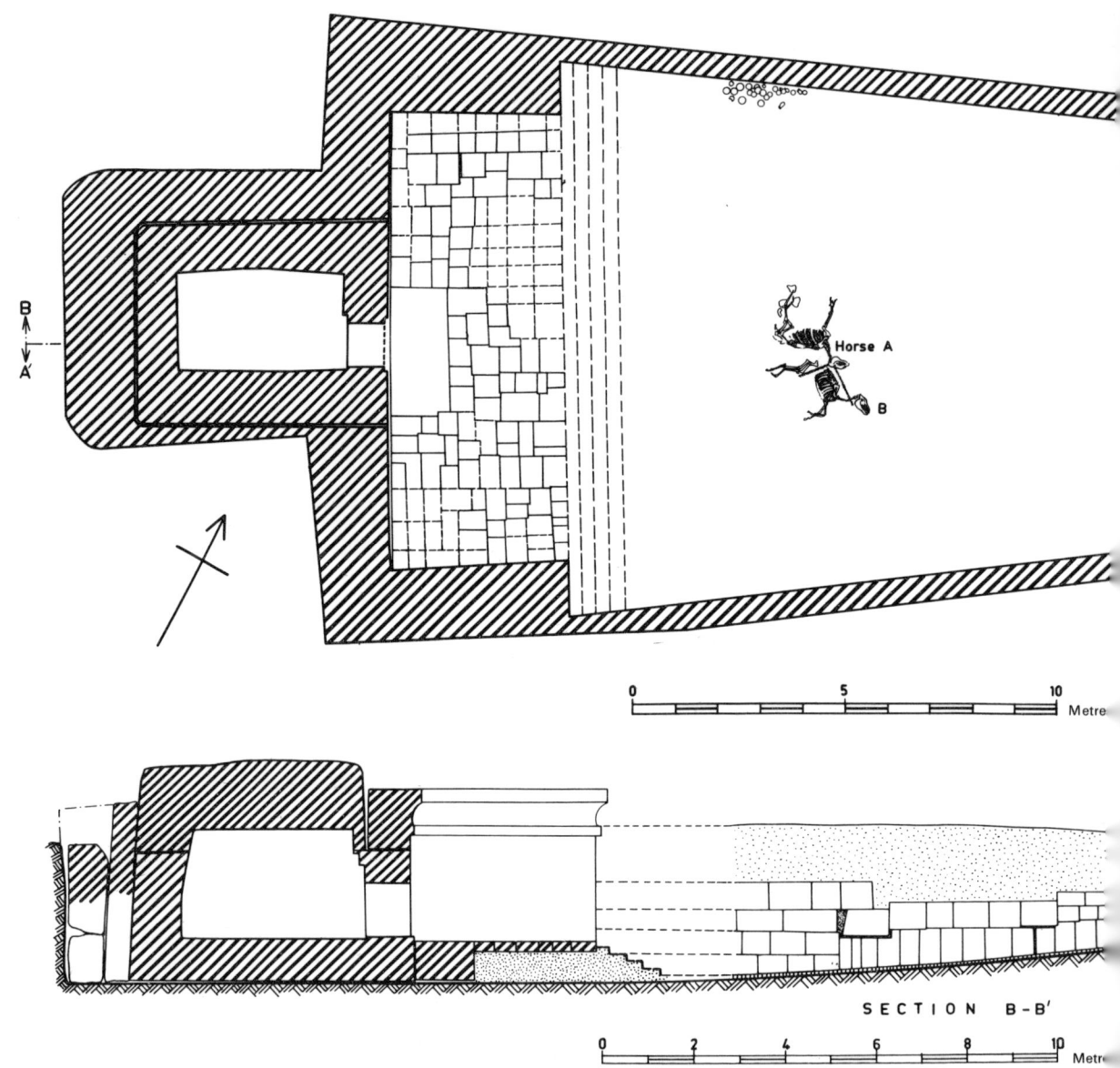

problem, and the architecture of this megalithic building could be analyzed correctly even before the new excavation. There were clearly two periods in its construction, a fact which previous investigators failed to recognize and which created much confusion when they tried to present it as a single architectural unit. We traced a rectangular area in front of the east entrance to the vaulted chamber where, we reckoned, must be concealed a dromos

*8 Reconstructed plan of the first period of Tomb 50; it shows the funerary chamber, the paved propylaeum and the large dromos with the skeletal remains of two horses on its floor*

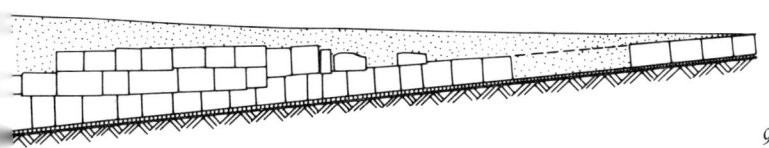

*9 Section of Tomb 50, showing the structures of the first period, with the large monoliths of the funerary chamber and the propylaeum. The sides of the dromos were dressed with ashlar blocks*

of the same size as that in front of this chamber. Excavation bore this out: a large dromos with its side walls built of well dressed ashlar blocks was found, with a cemented sloping floor of about the same width as that of the vaulted chamber. The skeletons of two horses were found on the floor, and this proved beyond doubt that here was originally another tomb of the same period and type as Tomb 47.

Plate 21; *Fig. 8*

Plate 22

The following is a description of the original building, based on the evolution of its architecture and its use.

The tomb was constructed in a large ditch dug in the clayey rock, aligned east-west and measuring 39.50m. in length and 15m. in width. The chamber, situated in the western part, was carved out of two very large blocks, placed on top of one another. The lower block measured about 4.70m. × 2.80m. × 6.20m., and the upper block which formed the roof, 5.00m. × 3.40m. × 2.00m. The chamber inside was rectangular, 4.10m. × 2.40m. with a gable roof 2.40m. high. In front of the chamber was a spacious propylaem in the shape of the Greek letter Π: the façade, represented by the horizontal line of the letter, measured 10.65m., the two vertical wings, represented by the two uprights, 4.00m. each. The height of the walls of the propylaeum was 3.40m. A cornice of the same style as that of Tombs 1, 2 and 47 decorated the upper part of the three walls of the propylaeum. Its floor was paved with stone slabs, but at the place where one would expect to find the staircase leading up to it from the dromos, a later cut could be seen which will shortly be explained. In front of the propylaeum there was the aforementioned dromos, with its sloping floor, 28m. long, and increasing in width from 6.85m. at its entrance to 13m. as it sloped down towards the propylaeum.

On the floor of the dromos near the end of its slope the skeletons of two yoked horses were found. Traces of the impressions left in the soil by the wood of the yoke and the pole could be clearly discerned. As in the case of Tomb 47, however, no other traces of a vehicle (obviously detached for burial) were found. In an undisturbed part of the filling of the dromos a deposit of juglets and shallow bowls dating to the early seventh century BC was found on the floor. There are indications that there were two burial periods in this tomb, but it is not easy to determine whether this pottery belonged to the first or to the second burial.

There was a major change in the architecture of the tomb which, like most built tombs of the same period in the necropolis, was discovered and re-used by the Romans. But whereas other tombs (*e.g.* Tomb 79) were re-used for burials, this one received different

*The Age of Exuberance*

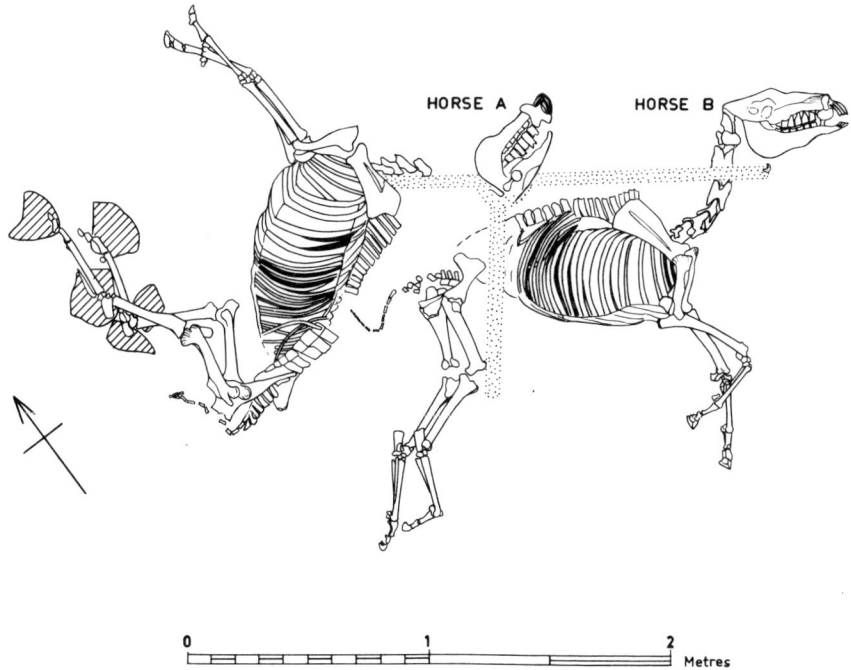

10   *Skeletal remains of two horses lying on the floor of the dromos of Tomb 50. The wood of the chariot's yoke and pole has left its impression in the soil*

treatment. The chamber must have been completely emptied, as well as the propylaeum and a small area in front of it, but in the dromos a layer of filling about 50cm. deep was left, so as to be on the same level with the threshold of the entrance to the new building. This is why the skeletons of the horses were preserved. The steps of the propylaeum were removed and a wall was built parallel to the façade of the chamber tomb. Thus the propylaeum was transformed into a four-sided chamber and a vaulted roof was constructed over it. The stone pavement of the former served as the floor of the new chamber, which had its entrance in the middle of the new east wall. It is interesting to note that for the new constructions stones must have been taken from a nearby built tomb of the same period, and it is not improbable that this was Tomb 47, which the Romans must also have discovered. The cornice of the propylaeum, and some blocks were also used outside, on the wall

*Fig. 14*

*Fig. 12*

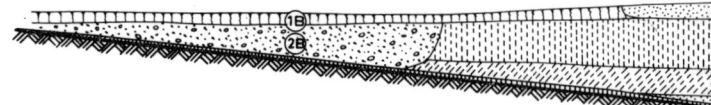

*11 Section of Tomb 50 showing the four periods (I–IV) in the history of the structure; one may see distinctly the vaulted chamber of Period II and the various arrangements at its entrance during the ensuing periods. The various layers of soil in the filling of the dromos correspond to its four periods*

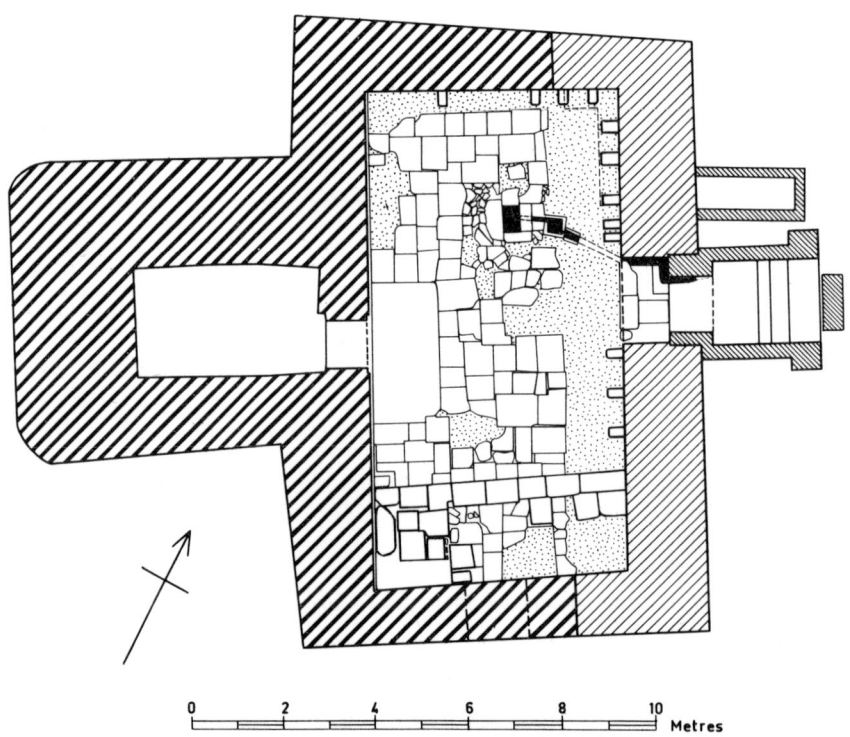

*12 Plan of the two chambers of Tomb 50 showing Period I (thick hatching) and the ensuing Periods II and III, during which the vaulted chamber was constructed with its complicated entrance to the east*

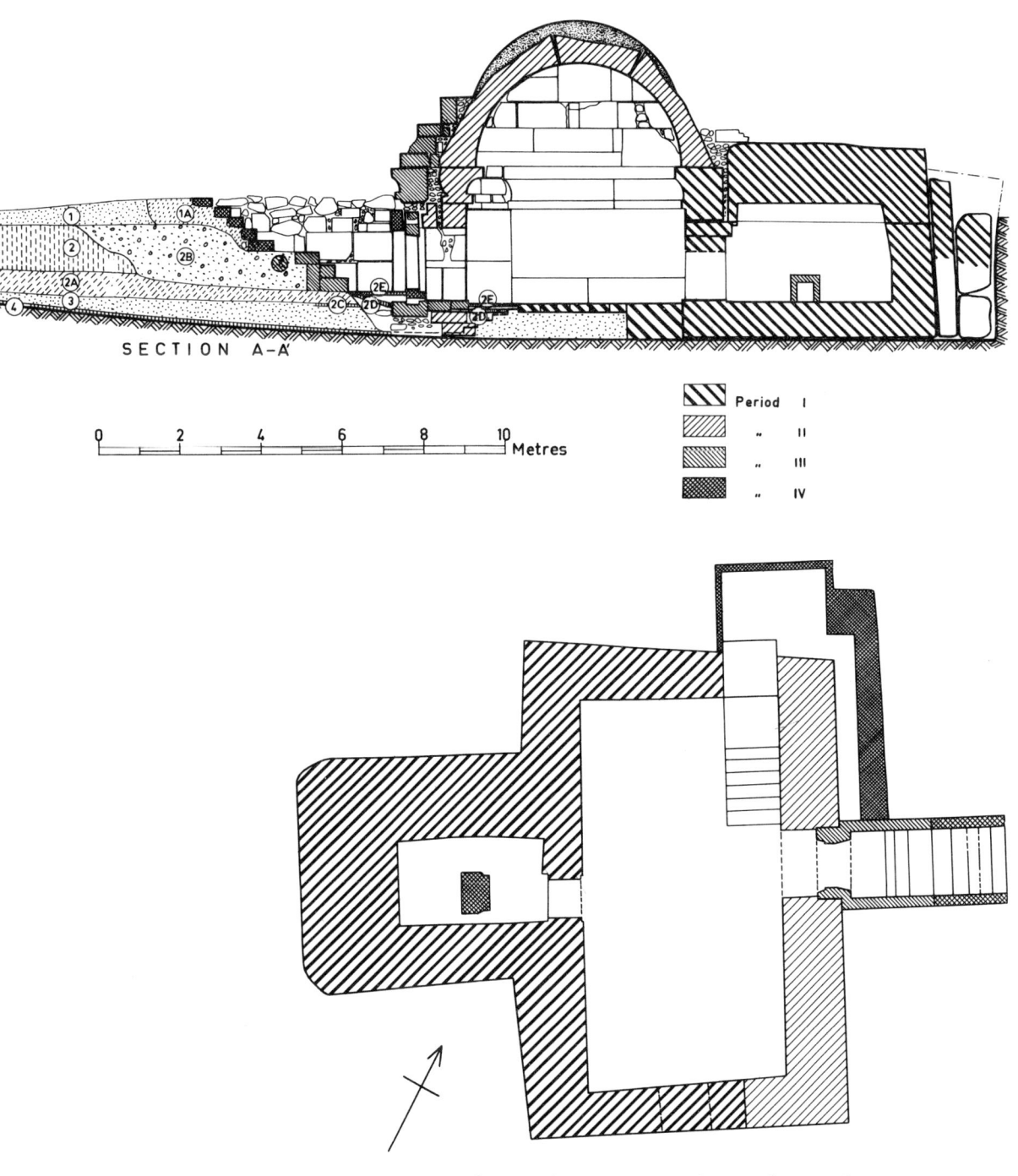

13 Plan of the chambers of Tomb 50 showing Periods I–IV; the last period (latticed) shows a boundary wall on the right-hand side on entering the vaulted chamber

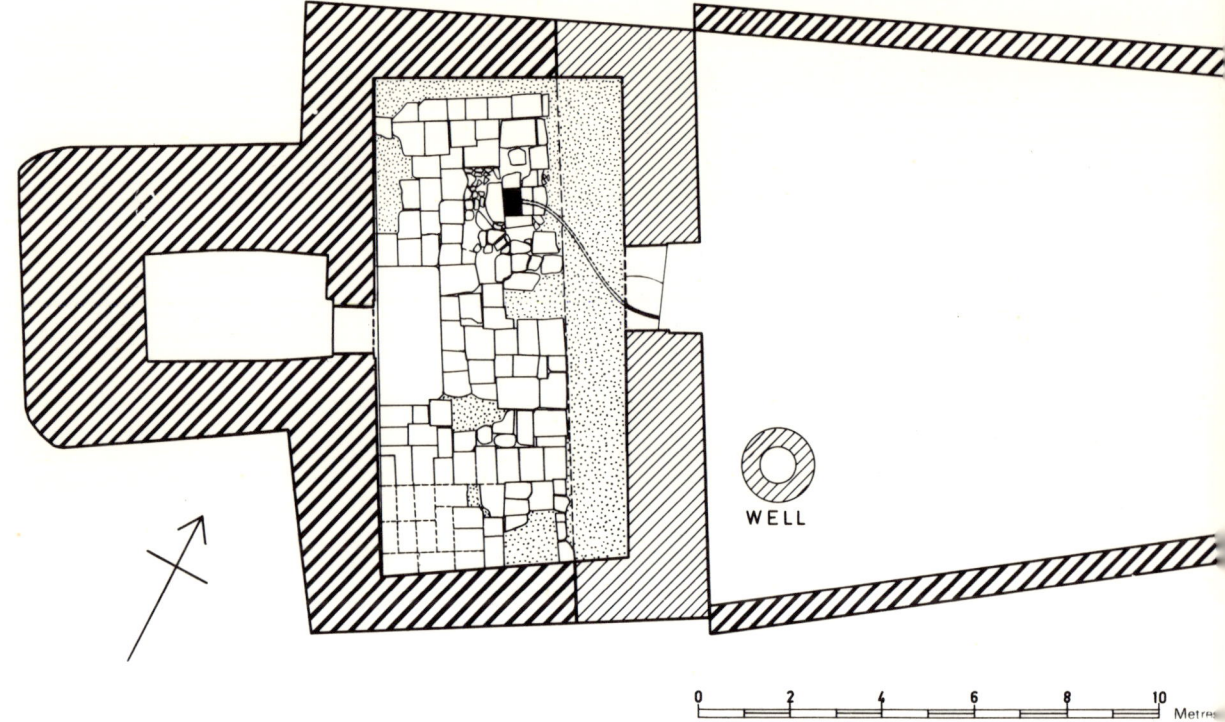

of the façade of the vaulted chamber. In style and in the size of the stones used, the new constructions differ materially from those of the original built tomb. The cornice – assuming that it belongs to Tomb 47, as the small fragment found in its dromos suggests – also differs from that of Tomb 50. Outside the entrance a kind of a new propylaeum was constructed, with columns and cornices of the Augustan period which certainly belonged to a public building of the city-site of Salamis, destroyed during the earthquake of AD 77. The purpose of this new building is not certain. There was no sign of a burial in it, but it might well have been used as a sanctuary or *heroon* for the dead.

The earthquakes which destroyed the Roman city of Salamis in the fourth century AD must have caused the collapse of the Roman propylaeum in front of the vaulted chamber. The area round the chamber was soon transformed into a burial ground from the second half of the fourth century until the seventh century AD. At the same time the entrance to the new chamber was furnished with a portcullis door, a large slab of hard limestone measuring

*Fig. 13*

14 *Plan of Tomb 50 showing Periods I and II; during the second period (thin hatching) the propylaeum was closed by a wall on the eastern side and it was vaulted in order to form a large roofed chamber in front of the small funerary chamber*

2.25m. × 1.20m. × 0.35m., which could be lowered and raised from the outside by means of a horizontal bar cut out of the slab itself. Are we to suppose that this new arrangement was associated with the transformation of this building into a prison, in which a local saint named Catherine suffered martyrdom and was buried? Even if we dismiss the idea that this saint is the great St Catherine, we should not disregard tradition completely; there may be an element of truth in it since the place has such a venerable antiquity (it was first mentioned in the fourteenth century AD). During the medieval period this building was used as a chapel and it continues to serve this purpose down to the present day. It is interesting to see how the site, as often occurs with ancient buildings, never lost its sanctity from the seventh century BC onwards. There are several remarkable instances of this in Cyprus, some of which, if carefully explored may lead to major discoveries. The fact, for example, that the most prominent part of the site where the Paphian temple of Aphrodite was built is now occupied by a Byzantine chapel may not be completely fortuitous.

I The two bronze cauldrons found in the dromos of Tomb 79, which is of the eighth century BC. One of them (left) is decorated with eight protomes of griffins and four double-faced bird-men, all round the rim. It stands on an iron tripod. The second cauldron much damaged, is decorated with three protomes of bulls on the rim below each of the two loop handles, and a plaque with an engraved head of Hathor attached on the shoulder below the rim (*see* Plate 40)

II Skeletons of horses and remains of chariot Δ, found on the floor of the dromos of Tomb 79 from the second burial. The horses trappings consisted of bronze blinkers, head-bands, breast-plates and side pendant ornaments, and they had iron bits in their mouths. The yoke was decorated with four bronze banners (*cf.* Plate 26). The chariot box was divided into two compartments, one for the warrior and the other for the charioteer

III Detail of the head of one of the skeletons of horses of chariot Δ, with bronze gear *in situ*

I

II

III

*The Age of Exuberance*

**Tomb 3** is a burial covered by a large tumulus of earth,[44] dominating the whole plain of the Salamis cemetery, and lying within the small area of the built 'royal' tombs described above. The tumulus, with a diameter of about 60m. at the base and 10m. in height (originally it must have been higher), was challenging for the looter and the archaeologist alike. The tomb underneath it was robbed some time in the nineteenth century by tunnelling, and so in 1896, when a British Museum expedition, following the same methods, reached the chamber, they found it empty. The sketches which they published, accompanied by a text of a few lines, show that they cut one of their tunnels along the filling of the dromos down to the floor, thus inadvertently destroying without recognizing anything which was lying on it, as we shall see below. The only object which they recorded was a sherd inscribed on both sides in the Cypriote syllabic script, the text of which was at that time erroneously interpreted as referring to an oracle.[45]

The tomb was built in more or less the same fashion as those already described. Set in the west side of a ditch 29m. long and about 6m. wide dug into the clayey rock was a rectangular chamber made of well dressed ashlar blocks of hard limestone. The chamber measured 2.93m. × 2.38m. and had a saddle roof at a height of 2.83m. The floor was covered with slabs of limestone. In front of the entrance there was a small propylaeum in the shape of the Greek letter Π, as in the other built tombs but smaller in size, being 3.34m. wide, 2.18m. deep, and 3.40m. high. The floor of the propylaeum was paved with stone slabs which had been removed by the looters in their search for the tomb. The stones inside the chamber have a well smoothed surface, but they are rather roughly carved on the façade of the propylaeum, where the tool marks are clearly visible. A large slab in the shape of a flanged rectangular stopper closed the entrance to the chamber, and was fixed to it with gypsum. The looters, however, broke into the chamber from above by removing a slab of the roof.

The sloping dromos of the tomb, 24.6m. long and 5.20m. wide near the propylaeum, narrows to 4.70m. near the entrance. For a length of about 9 metres next to the propylaeum its walls are lined

*Fig. 15*

*Plate 23*

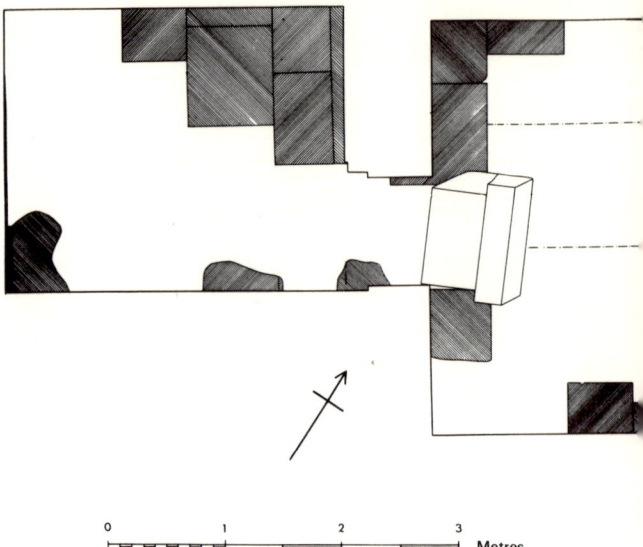

*15 Plan of Tomb 3 showing what was left of the chamber (left) and part of the long dromos. On the floor of the dromos are traces of the two vehicles, the skeletal remains of horses and the tomb gifts which survived the destruction caused by tunnelling in 1896*

with large sun-dried mud-bricks of pinkish colour, which add to its monumental character.

The tomb was used for a single burial, after which the tumulus of earth was piled above it.

Though the 1896 tunnel had swept away everything that was lying on the floor within it, yet enough survived on either side, in the undisturbed filling of the dromos, to make the excavation a worth-while undertaking. The skeletons of four horses, though badly mutilated by the tunnel digging, were found lying on the floor, each pair in association with a vehicle. Of the first of these, which was a war chariot, substantial remains survived, but of the second, a hearse, only a few metal parts were found in the soil thrown outside the 1896 tunnel, which show that it was of the same type as that of Tomb 2. The body of the war chariot was small, made of wood and leather which left their impressions in the soil. The rear edge was resting on the axle; its front was convex and almost oval. The pole consists of two parts, the lower of which springs from below the chariot box and is attached to the axle, the upper from the front of the chariot body. The two meet to form a

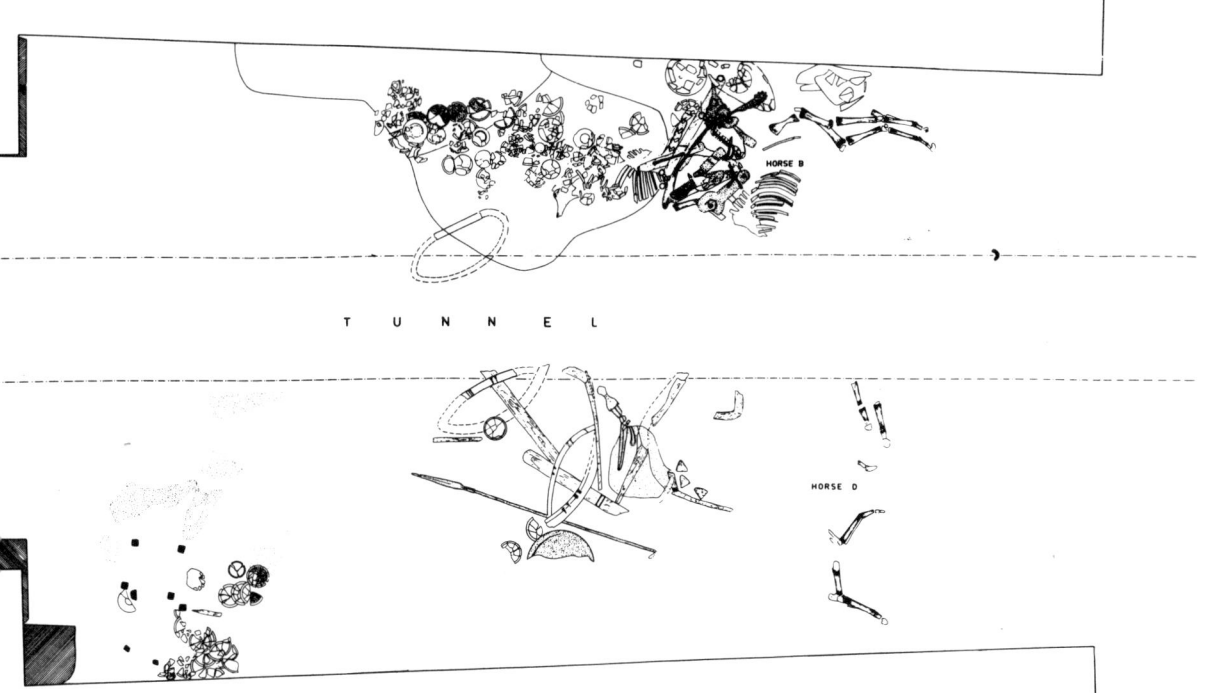

triangle which was fastened with leather straps for better suspension. The leather had left a brown stain on the soil. This type recalls the Mycenaean chariot as depicted on Mycenaean 'chariot' craters of the fourteenth and thirteenth centuries BC. The wheels, one of which left sufficiently good impressions in the soil to be cast in plaster, had a diameter of 85cm. with eight spokes but no metal tyres on the rims; the rims themselves consisted of four curved pieces of wood which retained their iron nails and iron joints. The hub was of wood and turned round the axle; no traces of a linch-pin were found.

The chariot box, as well as the axle and pole, had suffered serious damage through the pressure of the filling of the dromos and the tumulus (the box was almost folded double), or from the 1896 tunnel, so no exact dimensions of the various parts of the chariot could be obtained; but there is no doubt that it was a war chariot. On either side of the box there was a quiver of wood and leather (?) the iron arrow-heads of which were found in bundles. Part of a bronze circular shield and an iron spear-head were found next to the chariot box. The wooden shaft of the spear had left its im-

*Salamis*

Plate 25

pression in the soil, and its total length could thus be calculated at 2.18m. Inside the chariot box was found an iron sword, 92cm. long, with traces of its sheath of wood and leather. It had a rounded pommel of perishable material, which had also left its impression in the soil. It was fastened on the tang with silver-headed bronze rivets. This is obviously the type of 'silver-studded' sword described by Homer, several other examples of which are known from Cyprus.[46] The ivory toggle of the sheath has been found, with traces of its leather straps. This recalls the toggles which appear on Assyrian reliefs hanging from the belts of prisoners who had to surrender their swords.[47] An impression in the soil next to one of the two quivers suggests a double curved wooden bow.

There is no doubt that the remains of this vehicle are of extreme importance for the better understanding of the war chariot of the seventh century BC of which several representations appear on Assyrian reliefs and elsewhere, and several descriptions are to be found in the Homeric poems.

Of the second vehicle, the hearse, parts of the yoke and pole have been identified (always by their impressions left in the soil); these show how the pole was attached to the yoke by means of leather straps fastened on wooden attachments at the lower part of the pole, exactly as in primitive carts of to-day.

Plate 26

On the upper part of the pole there were found bronze standards, of which only three survived, fixed on wooden shafts, on either side of each horse's head. Shaped like nine-petalled flowers, they are flat, 54cm. high and quite heavy; these, together with the other bronze gear which we shall describe below, were obviously used for the funerary ceremony alone. Such objects appear on the yoke of the gold chariot model from the Oxus Treasure and on clay models from Cyprus which can now be interpreted correctly after the discovery of the actual objects which they represent.[48] The horses had iron bits, and blinkers and head bands of bronze which were preserved *in situ*, as well as the bronze breast-plates and disc-shaped side pendant ornaments such as appear above the forelegs of horses on Assyrian reliefs and on terracotta chariot groups from Cyprus. They are perforated along their border, and probably had tassels hanging from them, as did the breast-plates. Their inside surface must have been dressed with leather so as to protect the animal's skin when they were worn. The horses also had bronze bells, an example of which was found on the floor at some distance from one of the animals. This heavy and glittering gear must have added appreciably to the pomp and luxury of the funerary ritual in honour of the warrior occupant of the tomb.

On the floor of the dromos considerable quantities of pottery were found. These included large amphorae, dishes and small jars. Below the handle of one of the amphorae a painted inscription in the Cypriote syllabary was found which reads in Greek 'of olive oil', *i.e.* 'an amphora of olive oil'. This is of particular importance for students of Homeric archaeology, as it evokes most directly the passage in the *Iliad* where the already cited funeral of Patroklos is described.[49] The jars, most of them with their lids on, are of a type which is used to-day in Cyprus for storing honey, and may have had the same function in antiquity. Most of the dishes contained egg-shells – the connection of eggs with funerary ritual throughout the Mediterranean area is well known. Impressions of wood were traced on a partly undisturbed portion of the filling of the dromos near the propylaeum and these included the four legs of at least one chair or stool. There were also next to it stains of purple and pink colour on the soil, evidently from pieces of coloured cloth.

Plate 24

On the floor of the dromos were traces of a large pyre on which the corpse must have been cremated. We have already mentioned that the tomb was used for only one burial, which took place about 600 BC to judge by the pottery, when a large tumulus of earth (the Homeric *tymbos*) composed of horizontal layers of soil, was built above it. The construction of the tumulus was carefully planned: a circular perimeter was traced with the propylaeum more or less in the centre, from which small radiating walls of rubble were constructed, in such a way that the top of the tumulus was directly above the centre of the circle at the base. These walls were heightened as the tumulus rose. There must have been ten such radiating walls, four of which survive in our sections. When the tumulus had

*Salamis*

reached a height of about 4m. above the floor level of the propylaeum a beehive construction of sun-dried bricks was erected, supported on radiating walls of mud-brick, with a diameter at the base of about 9.40m. Only small parts of it survived the various disturbances of the tumulus caused by repeated tunnelling. The top of this structure, which might have been visible, is aligned vertically with the propylaeum beneath, not with the chamber. This may have been done to deceive prospective looters, a method which is known from similarly constructed tumuli in Asia Minor.[50] The beehive construction of mud-bricks, which had no practical function whatsoever, may be regarded as a remnant of a Mycenaean tradition in tomb architecture, the tholos tomb, of which examples have recently come to light in the nearby Late Bronze Age town of Enkomi.

We have derived a wealth of information from Tomb 3, in spite of the fact that it was repeatedly looted in the past. The impression of the war chariot with all its apparatus, the richly caparisoned horses, the architecture of the tumulus, all these are of extreme importance for the student of Near Eastern and Homeric archaeology.

**Tombs 19 and 31,** two smaller and less monumental structures, were found at a short distance west of the tumulus.[51] Of these, Tomb 19 had been looted. It was constructed in the same manner as the larger built tomb, with the chamber situated at the one end of a ditch dug in the clayey rock, and a sloping dromos at the other end. But the construction of the chamber was rather crude, with roughly shaped stones. In a corner on the floor the burnt bones of the dead were found in a small pit.[52] On the floor of the dromos the skeletal remains of an ass were found; there must have been two originally, but the second one was removed at the time of a second burial in the chamber. The scanty fragments of pottery found on the floor of the tomb suggest a seventh-century date. The second tomb, No. 31, of the same architectural plan as Tomb 19, was found almost intact. It had a rectangular chamber, built of irregular blocks of limestone and measuring 3.50m. × 1.80m. The roof, at a height of 1.60m. from the floor, was flat and composed of long slabs of schist, as in the case of Tomb 1 described above. The skeletons of

*Fig. 16*

*Figs. 17–19*

Plate 30

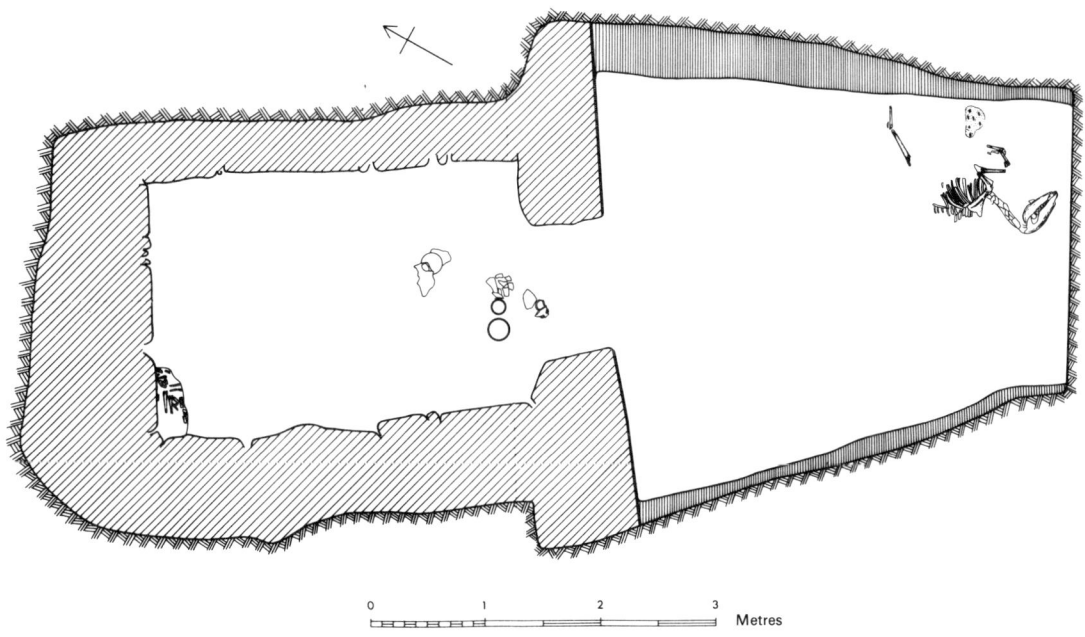

*16 Plan of Tomb 19 showing the built chamber (left) and the dromos (right), with the skeletal remains of an ass lying on its floor. In a corner of the chamber, in a pit, were the incinerated remains of the dead owner*

two asses (unyoked and without any gear, as in the case of Tomb 19) were found lying on the floor of the dromos. On the floor of the chamber an amphora was found half-buried in the ground, containing cremated human remains. The pyre on which the body was burnt had left its traces on the floor of the dromos. In a pit on the floor of the chamber large numbers of thin gold sheet diadems were found; most of these are plain but some have an embossed decoration depicting a chariot group or a winged sphinx or a rosette. Two burials have been identified in this chamber; one had followed close upon the other, sometime in the first half of the seventh century BC. The pottery is rich in shape and decoration.

Plate 29

Plate 28

Plate 27

Plates 31, 32

It is interesting to note that in these less important built tombs asses and not horses were sacrificed, without vehicles and without any gear. They may not, therefore be considered as 'royal', though they differ from the simple chamber tombs of the ordinary folk. They may belong to an intermediate class of noblemen or wealthy citizens of Salamis.

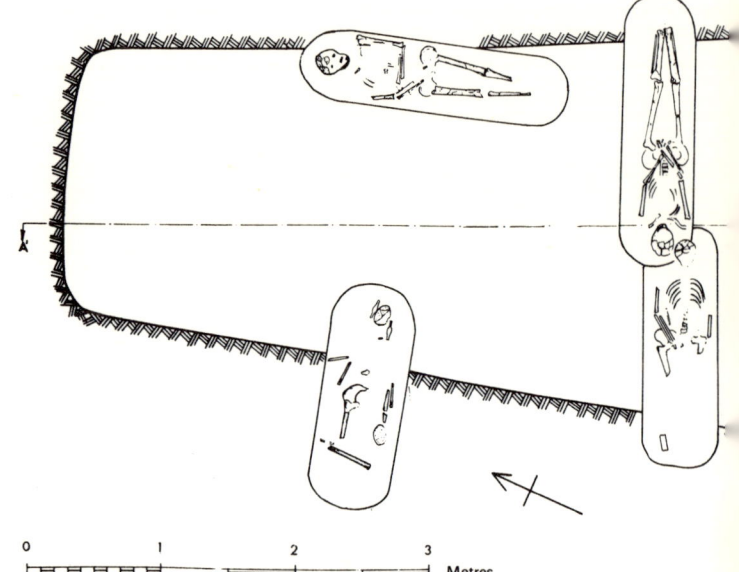

17  Plan showing the upper levels of Tomb 31. On the right are the slabs of the roof of the chamber, on the left the skeletal remains from later burials within shallow pits, above the filling of the dromos

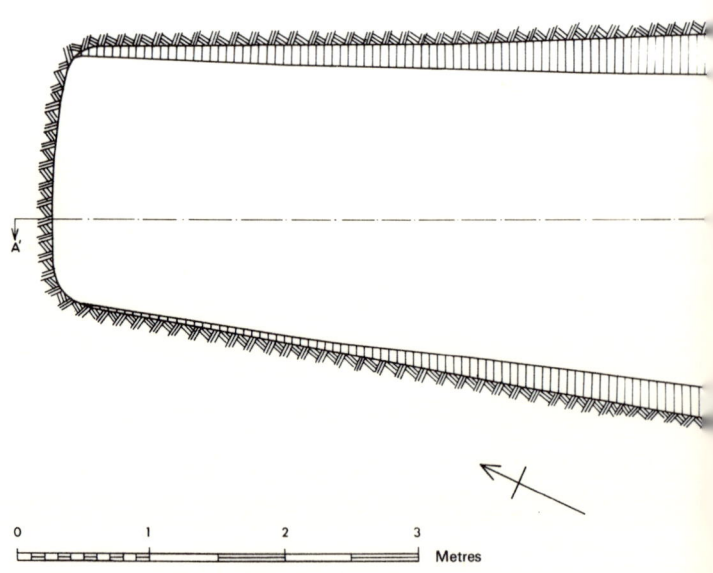

18  Plan of Tomb 31 showing objects in situ within the funerary chamber (right) and skeletal remains of two asses lying in a symmetrical position on the floor of the dromos

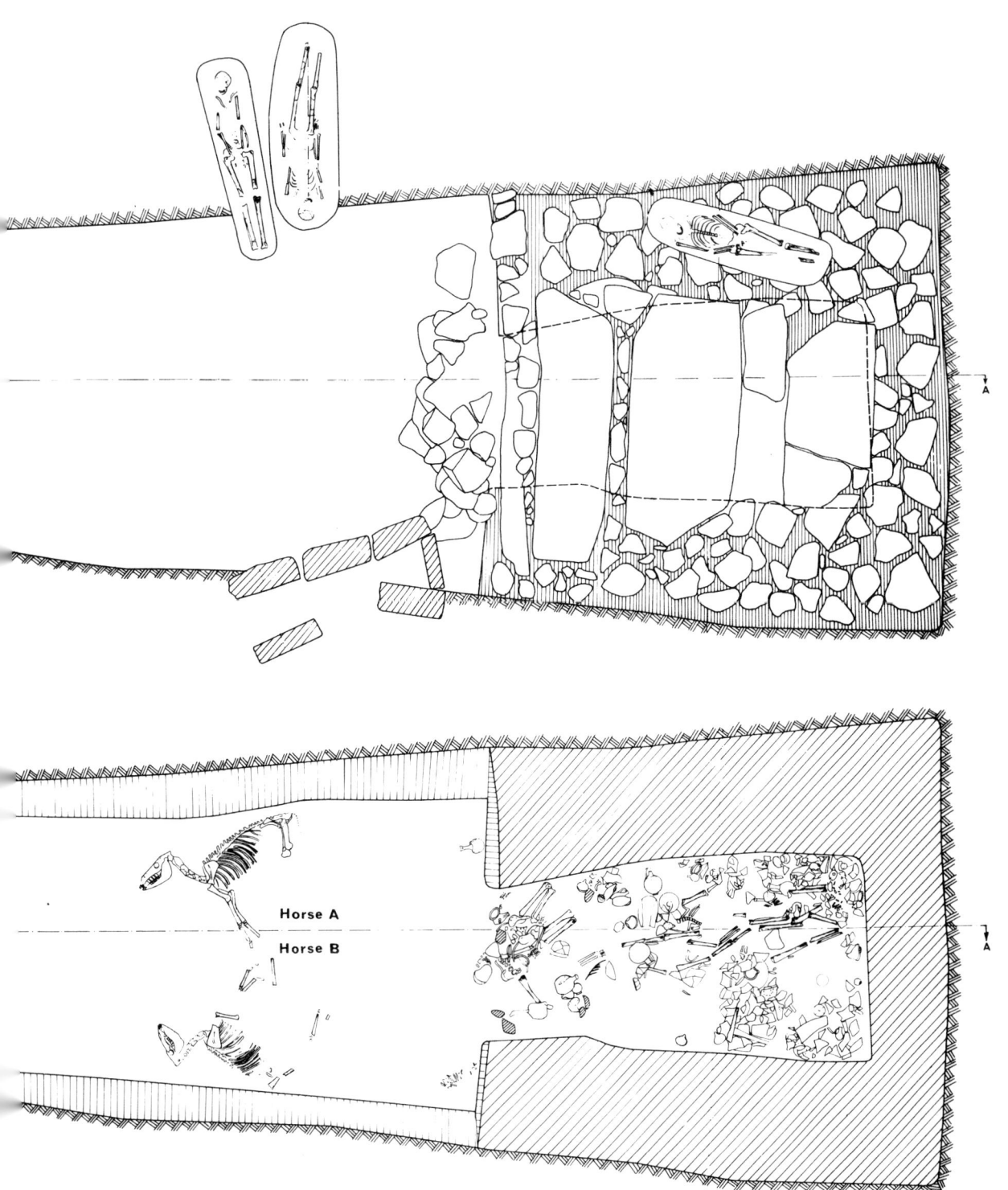

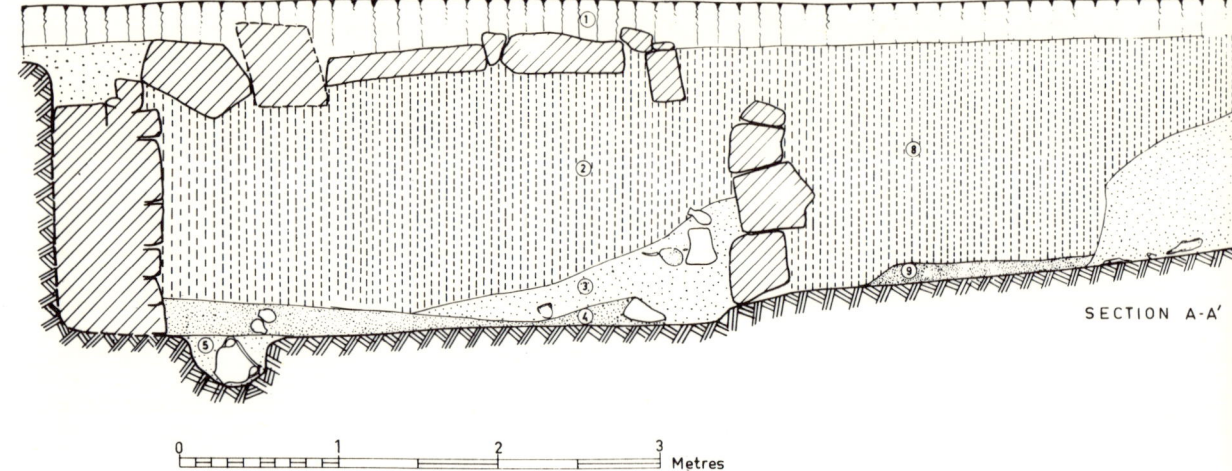

SECTION A-A'

**Tomb 79** is one of the richest ever found in Cyprus and was excavated in 1966.[53] Like almost all the other built tombs in the necropolis of Salamis this too had been looted. In fact its chamber was re-used during the Roman period (second century AD) and the nineteenth-century looters must have found only the Roman burials in it. The tomb was first seen by Ohnefalsch-Richter during his investigations at Salamis, and it is referred to by Salomon Reinach in his article in *Chroniques d'Orient* for the year 1885, in which he describes Ohnefalsch-Richter's archaeological activities in Cyprus. He gives the measurements of the monolithic roof of the tomb – at least what was visible on the surface without excavation. It was at that time already ascertained that the chamber of the tomb had been looted, and was, therefore, of no importance. By excavating the chamber we partly verified this assertion. The chamber, built, as was that of Tomb 50, of two very large blocks of stone, was rectangular in shape, measuring 3.20m. × 2.40m., and had a gable roof 1.80m. above the floor. During the Roman period niches were carved in the north and south walls in order to provide space for sarcophagi. Two further niches had been cut into the west wall, thus penetrating it, and it was through these openings that the investigators of 1885 were able to see that the chamber had been looted. Remains of clay sarcophagi were found in the niches and

Plate 34

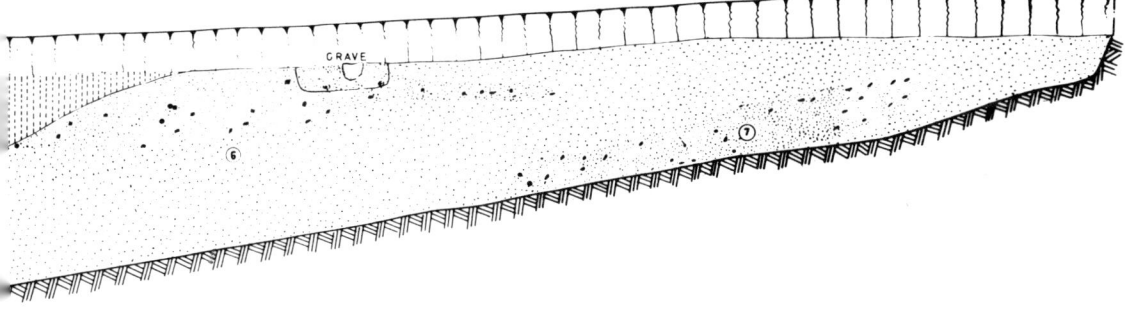

*19 Section of Tomb 31 showing the filling of the chamber (left) and the dromos (right). Layers 6 and 7 in the filling of the dromos belong to the first burial period; layer 8 belongs to the subsequent period*

enough ceramic material and lamps to point to a Roman date for these new arrangements.

The main purpose of our excavation, however, was the dromos east of the chamber, and here we concentrated our efforts for three months with the following results. A small staircase, crudely built with stones, was found in front of the stomion, obviously constructed for the re-use of the chamber in Roman times. This had disturbed a relatively small part of the filling of the dromos, but the greater part of it was found intact.

The façade of the chamber, constructed of well-dressed blocks of hard limestone, formed a rectangular Π-shaped recess, 7.00m. × 3.20m. and 2.40m. high, with the stomion in the middle and turning at right angles at each outer end to join the side walls of the dromos which were also constructed of well dressed ashlar blocks. The floor of the recess in front of the stomion was paved with limestone slabs. The total width of the façade was 12.80m. and this corresponds also to the maximum width of the dromos which narrows near the entrance to 9m. The total length of the dromos is 16.80m. The floor was covered with a concrete cement and sloped down towards the stomion.

The stratification of the filling of the dromos showed on examination that there were two burial periods in the tomb. During

Plate 33

the first burial, which may be dated by the pottery to the end of the eighth century BC, two vehicles were placed in the dromos, a chariot and a hearse, one drawn by four, the other by two quadrupeds (horses?). The skeletal remains of these animals, however, were thoroughly disturbed during the second burial – which, as we shall see below, followed a few years after the first – and were found broken and scattered in the filling of the dromos which was poured back after the second burial. The vehicles themselves were put on the south side of the dromos: the chariot with the edge of its two poles touching the south wall of the dromos, and the hearse just behind it to the east. The chariot could still be wheeled away in perfect condition (this is why we assume that there was only a very short interval between the two periods) while the hearse had lost its wheels and pole.

The chariot, registered as chariot 'B', had two poles 2.90m. long and about 7cm. in diameter, passing below the sides of the chariot box and projecting 18cm. beyond it at the back. The poles, as well as all the wooden parts of the chariot, had left their distinct impressions in the soil, which have been carefully measured, photographed and drawn. Both ends of the poles were protected by bronze caps. They rested on the axle, to which they were fixed with two large iron nails. At the back of each pole, on the part which was projecting beyond the chariot box an ovoid bronze disc hung vertically allowing the bronze cap of the terminal to show through. These discs are decorated in repoussé with a winged lion striding over a conquered, fallen enemy in the well-known Egyptian fashion. The disc is perforated all round its perimeter and was probably sewn on a plaque of another material (leather?) which has perished.

The axle, 2.90m. long and about 9cm. thick, passed below the back part of the chariot box, with the two poles set upon it. Each end of the axle was fitted with a bronze cap in the shape of a head of a sphinx with a broad collar rim all round the neck. Her eyes were inlaid with white paste. Inserted vertically through the neck of the sphinx and consequently through the axle, was an iron linch-pin, bearing at the top a bronze figurine of a fully armed soldier cast

*20 Bronze plaque found at the back of the pole of chariot B in Tomb 79. It is decorated in repoussé with a winged lion striding over an enemy, a well-known subject in Egyptian iconography. Ht: 32.7cm.*

hollow with a rattle inside it. One of these figurines was found on the floor, having become detached from the linch-pin, probably at the time of the filling of the dromos. The other one had already been detached when the chariot was wheeled away for the second burial, as it was found thrown in the corner of the propylaeum in a pile of bronze gear which belonged to the horses of this chariot. The total length of the linch-pin was 56cm. The figure itself, about 37cm. high, his eyes inlaid with blue paste, wears a foliated cuirass inlaid with blue paste, above a short chiton. He also wears a helmet with a semicircular crest terminating above the forehead in a disc, also inlaid with paste. The crest is perforated and must have held small feathers. Under his left arm he holds the pommel of a sword which is hanging from a belt across his torso. The glitter of the bronze, the polychromy of the inlaid paste and the rattle of the linch-pins must have added an impressive note to the solemn pomp of the funeral cortège when this vehicle was passing.

The two wheels on the chariot had a diameter of 90cm.; they had ten spokes, but no metal tyres. Ten pairs of iron nails were found all round the rim of the wheel, fixed cross-wise, one pair to every spoke. Each pair probably fixed together two curved pieces of wood to make a kind of a double rim. They were 5cm. in length with a flat head at both ends. There was ample space for the wooden hub of the wheel (16cm. maximum thickness) to move freely along the axle. The space between the axle end and the side of the chariot box is about 70cm.

The sides of the chariot box, as far as we could see from the pale, square-shaped stains left on the soil, were made of plaited osiers;[54] this must have been, therefore, a light chariot. Its dimensions have been calculated as 68cm. in width, 85cm. in depth and 44cm. in height. It had a convex front and was divided inside by a partition, possibly wooden, into two compartments, one for the charioteer and the other for the warrior, as on chariot models. At the back of this diaphragm there was a bronze tubular loop, 50cm. high, fixed to the floor of the box, and which those mounting the chariot could grip; it also served to hold the shield in place at the back of the chariot box. This is the first time that this object, which so often appears on clay chariot models from Cyprus, can be interpreted correctly. The yoke, 1.95m. long, was found placed across the terminals of the poles, along the south side wall of the dromos. It had at the top four bronze rings for the reins. At each end there were semicircular horn-shaped attachments of bronze, rectangular in section and turned upwards.

The second vehicle, registered as hearse 'Γ' (gamma) was not so well preserved as the chariot. It had lost its wheels, but enough was left to show that the body, which was richly decorated with bronze nails, had been attached to the axle in the same manner as for the hearse from Tomb 2. Round the floor of the hearse there were five bronze heads of lions, one at each of the four corners and one in the middle of the front side. They are hollow, with a socket at the top

## The Age of Exuberance

probably for the attachment of a post to support a canopy. These heads, 11cm. high, fitted into rectangular sockets in the wooden beams making up the floor of the hearse. Their rendering is very naturalistic and betrays Egyptian prototypes.

This particular hearse was more richly decorated than any hitherto found at Salamis, and exemplifies the wealth and luxury that characterized all the burial gifts of Tomb 79. Of the two other vehicles associated with the second burial, one is a hearse and the other a war chariot. They were both found in their original positions with the skeletons of the horses still lying *in situ*, though those of the hearse had been damaged by looters, being near the surface by the entrance of the dromos. The chariot, registered as chariot 'Δ' (delta), was a biga. Its chariot box, 90cm. wide, 72cm. long and 25cm. deep was divided into two compartments, one for the charioteer and the other for the warrior, as in chariot 'B'. The back of the chariot box was closed with a wooden plank which could be secured by detachable iron nails. The axle is 2.10m. long and about 10cm. in diameter. The wheels, however, were largely destroyed, probably by the weight of the filling of the dromos and the stones which were placed all round them. They seem to have been like those of chariot 'B', to judge by the ten pairs of nails which they had all round the rim and their ten spokes.

Plates II, III

The pole, 2.80m. long and 7cm. in diameter, had at the lower part of its terminal three small wooden attachments by which it could be fixed with leather straps to the yoke. These three projections enabled the pole to be adjusted in length so as to facilitate driving uphill or downhill respectively. The same principle is practised in farm carts of the present day. The pole passed beneath the chariot box and was fixed on the axle which ran below its rear. Just in front of the chariot box the pole clearly curves upwards to meet the level of the yoke.

The yoke, 1.64m. long and 6cm. in diameter, had at each end bronze horn-shaped terminals, rectangular in section and turned upwards, as for the yoke of chariot 'B'. At their point of attachment there were two iron plaques to prevent wear. On top of the yoke and at regular intervals were four bronze rings for the reins

IV–VI One of the most important pieces of ivory furniture found in the dromos of Tomb 79 was a throne (Plates VI and 42) which has now been reconstructed. Next to it, on the floor of the dromos, were two plaques of ivory carved on both sides in openwork; one (Plate IV) represents a composite lotus flower, incrusted with paste of blue and brown colour. The other (Plate V) represents a sphinx wearing the crowns of Upper and Lower Egypt. Its cloisons are gilded and inlaid with blue and brown paste. Both plaques have been placed tentatively between the arms and the seat of the throne

VII, VIII Among the carved ivory plaques found in the dromos of Tomb 79 were two groups which may have belonged to the decoration of an ivory bed. The first group consists of six small plaques forming one band; their carved decoration forms a frieze with the seated figure of the god Heh repeated six times, holding a branch of a palm tree from which hangs the Egyptian symbol *ankh*, suggesting good fortune. The relief decoration is partly gilded with a thin sheet of gold. The second group consists of six small plaques, decorated with three pairs of confronted sphinxes on either side of a stylized flower. The aprons and the head-dresses of the sphinxes, as well as the flowers, are gilded with thin sheets of gold. Similar carved ivory plaques have been found on other Near Eastern sites, *e.g.* Nimrud and Samaria, and may be considered as works of Egyptianizing Phoenician art.

IX A deep bowl, supported on a long terracotta stand, consisting of two opposed nude female figures with their backs against the stand, from Tomb 47. The bowl is decorated in the Bichrome technique, whereas the stand is decorated with red, black and white paint

X A deep bowl supported on a long stem with three draped female figures moulded around it from Tomb 23. The bowl is decorated all round with lotus flowers and buds, painted in black and yellow colours.

IV

V

VI

VII

VIII

IX                                  X

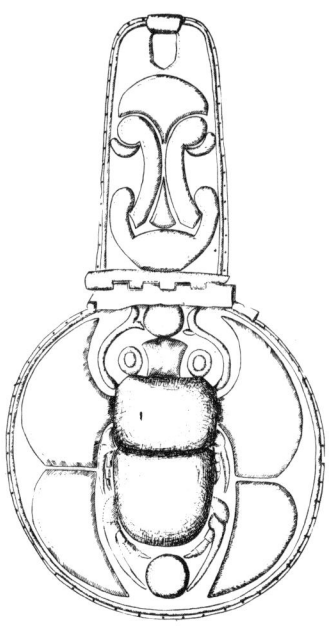

21 Bronze side pendant ornament found in situ *near one of the horses of chariot* Δ *in Tomb 79. It is decorated in repoussé with a beetle on the main disc. Ht: 45.5cm. Diam. of disc: 24.5cm.*

and there were also four bronze flower-shaped standards, of the type found on one of the chariots in Tomb 3; their height varies from 45 to 50cm. These were also found *in situ*, fixed to projections on the upper part of the yoke.

Vehicle 'A', of the second burial, was a hearse of a similar type to that of Tomb 2, but rather less well preserved than the other vehicles in Tomb 79, as, being very near the surface, it suffered together with the horses associated with it from the looters' excavations.

The horses associated with such richly decorated vehicles were correspondingly caparisoned. They had bronze blinkers and head bands, the upper part of the latter decorated with prominently curving crests, bronze breastplates decorated with a crescent in repoussé, and a side pendant ornament, one for each horse (only the outer flank of the horses being thus protected); these were decorated with large beetles in repoussé. The bits were of iron. All the above were found *in situ* and indicate the original position and function of this gear, often imperfectly represented in reliefs and other representations where three-dimensional rendering is lacking.

We have given a fairly detailed description of the chariots and hearses as it is very rarely that so much information about the con-

Plate III

Fig. 21

22 *Breastplate of bronze found together with other bronze gear near the façade of Tomb 79, belonging to the first burial period. It is decorated all over in two registers with 23 figures (human and animal) from Oriental mythology. Ht: 39.2cm.; width: 50.6cm.*

struction of actual vehicles comes to light. The excavation was carried out with care in order to extract the maximum evidence, but the interpretation of the various parts of the chariot given above should still be regarded as provisional – and this also applies to other descriptions of objects from this tomb – until all the material is cleaned and mended.

The gear of the horses of vehicle 'A' was also found but not all *in situ* since their skeletal remains had been disturbed.

The four horses of chariot 'B' and the two horses of the hearse 'Γ' were no doubt wearing their gear, and this has in fact been found, all piled up in a corner of the propylaem. During the second burial (which followed, as mentioned above, shortly after the first, when the vehicles 'B' and 'Γ' were removed) the metal gear of the horses was collected and put away, while the skeletal remains were destroyed. The bronze gear of the first burial is all very lavishly decorated in repoussé; we shall describe briefly the most important items.

a) *Breastplates*: Four of these are decorated in repoussé with 23 human and animal figures from oriental mythology. They include griffins, sphinxes, winged human figures holding situlae, scorpion men etc. The central part consists of a winged solar disc on top, a stylized 'Tree of Life' in the middle and a winged human figure holding a kid in his arms below. The width of these breastplates is 50cm. and their height 39–40cm.

b) *Side pendant ornaments*: Two of these have a disc decorated in repoussé with a winged nude Ishtar in the centre,[55] holding a lion in each hand and standing on the backs of two other lions. The lions above are being attacked by griffins and those below hold calves in their mouths. There is a winged solar disc and a Hathor's head above the head of Ishtar. Friezes of animals decorate the border of the disc and the hinged band above. The total height of the side pendant ornaments is 58cm. and the diameter 30cm.

c) *Head bands*: Of these, all crested, we mention only two kinds: four which are decorated in high repoussé with superimposed rows of couchant lions, uraei, nude human figures, and a winged solar disc; and two which are decorated in shallow repoussé with two figures of winged El, a solar disc and stylized lotus flowers. Their height is about 50cm. They all consist of two parts, hinged in the middle, and have a loop for attachment at the top.

*23, 24 Head bands of bronze found together with the breastplate in Fig. 22. Above, decorated in high repoussé with superimposed rows of figures including couchant lions, uraei, nude human figures and a winged solar disc; at the top it has a crest for the attachment of feathers. Ht: 51cm. Below, decorated in shallow repoussé with two superimposed figures of the winged god El and with a solar disc. Ht: 49.5cm. Tomb 79*

Salamis

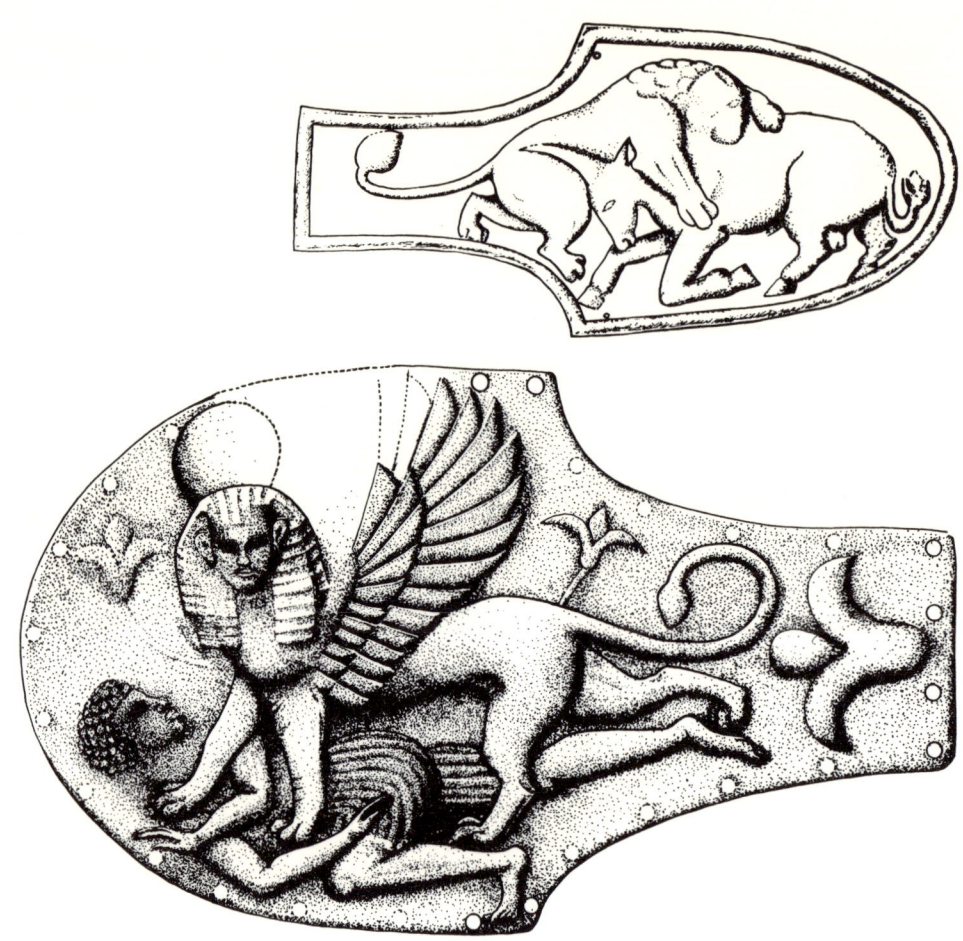

*25, 26  Two bronze blinkers found in Tomb 79 together with the objects in Figs. 22–25. Above, decorated in shallow repoussé with a lion attacking a kneeling bull. This was a favourite composition both in Oriental and Greek iconography of the Archaic period. Length: 22cm. Below, decorated in shallow repoussé with a winged sphinx striding over a fallen negro. Cf. Fig. 20 above. Length: 19.5cm.*

*Fig. 25*
*Fig. 26*

d) *Blinkers:* These are either plain or decorated with repoussé; their decoration takes the form of either a lion attacking a kneeling bull, or a winged sphinx striding over a prostrate negro. This decoration is similar to that on the bronze discs of chariot 'B' and is meant to represent the Egyptian Pharaoh striding over his enemies. The composition must have been adopted by Near Eastern art in a purely decorative context. The average length of the blinkers is 22–25cm.

*The Age of Exuberance*

All the pieces of the bronze gear described above are perforated round the entire border; they were probably sewn on leather in order to avoid chafing the animal's skin. Some of them must have also been decorated with tassels.

In addition to these harness ornaments we may also mention bronze bells and belts which were found on the pile of gear and which may also have belonged to the horses of the first burial.

We shall not attempt at this stage to make a stylistic analysis of these objects and determine their origin.[56] Though similar objects are known from elsewhere in Cyprus, the decoration of these is unique, and points to the art of the Near East, probably North Syria. One may also find elements in their decoration which recall the art of Urartu, but it is hard to assign to them any specific style. In a copper-producing country like Cyprus there may well have been artists, Cypriots or foreigners, who were producing such objects for the courts of the local kings and nobles copying Near Eastern prototypes.

There is no doubt that the richly decorated chariots and hearses, combined with the lavishly ornamented horses – let alone their colourful caparisons – must have offered a spectacle of extraordinary pomp and luxury.

Of the warrior's armour the only objects which survived are a large bronze spear-head and the hemispherical umbo of a silver shield, with the outer surface gilded. All round the rim the umbo is perforated for fixing on to the leather surface of the shield.

An extraordinary object found in the dromos of Tomb 79 near the north wall of the propylaeum, and obviously belonging to the first burial, was a bronze cauldron standing on an iron tripod base. The cauldron is 51cm. high, with a diameter at the mouth (deformed by pressure) of *c.* 65cm. and at the widest point of 94cm. The height of the tripod was 62cm., making the total height of the cauldron including attachments and tripod 125cm. The vessel was beaten out, with a very thick rim; all round it, on the shoulder and just below the rim, there are eight griffin protomes, fixed to it with rivets, which were cast by the *cire perdue* ('lost wax') method. The griffins have a flat crest on top of their heads which was cast

Plates 40, I
Fig. 27

# Salamis

separately. The total height of these protomes is 23cm. and they are plain, except for a zig-zag engraved decoration on a narrow collar round the neck.

There are also four more attachments on the shoulder of the cauldron, each arranged symmetrically between two pairs of griffins. They are made of several parts, some beaten and others cast separately, and represent bearded bird-men or sphinxes, with broad wings which are attached to the shoulder of the cauldron. The griffin on either side of the bird-men is rivetted to the wings. The body and legs are decorated with a scale pattern in repoussé; the head has two faces, one facing outwards, the other inwards. The details of the head are either incised or worked in repoussé and there is a double crest resting on the curly hair of the head. The feathers of the wings are rendered by means of incisions. The height of the head (without the body) is 18cm. whilst the total height of the bird-men is 36cm.

The tripod is made of beaten iron rods: there is a double ring at the top on which the cauldron rests (diameter 45cm.). Each leg consists of three rods of which the central one terminates in an anthemium and lily. They join towards the bottom and terminate in an animal's hoof cast in bronze.

Such cauldrons decorated with griffin protomes are known from Etruria and Greece, but they are very rare in the Near East.[57] We know of a number of bronze cauldrons from Altintepe, Toprakkale, Gordion and elsewhere, which are decorated round the rim usually with bull and siren attachments but not with griffin protomes. The Salamis cauldron is not only extraordinary in itself, as a work of art, with more protomes round its rim than any other known specimen, but it will help those studying the ultimate origin of this type of cauldron which derived no doubt from the Orient and became a favourite in the Aegean and Etruria.

Plate 40

A second bronze cauldron, very much corroded, was lying next to the first one. It is of a different type, with a high conical foot and two loop handles at the rim with three bull protomes below each handle, facing inwards. The vertical plate to which each handle is hooped is rivetted to the shoulder of the cauldron and bears a

*27 Two bronze cauldrons (right) and other bronze objects (left) including horses' gear and bronze flower-shaped standards from the pole of a chariot. They all belong to the first burial period and were piled up to one side, near the façade of the chamber, in order to make room for the second burial in Tomb 79*

representation in low relief of a Hathor's head below a winged solar disc and between two stylized palmettes. Its original height was probably about 75cm. and its diameter at the mouth is about 40cm.

Next to the pile of horse-gear from the first burial were two rather unusual iron objects, a pair of fire-dogs, and a bundle of twelve iron skewers bound together with two rings; there was a loop between the two rings for carrying. Both fire-dogs terminate in the prow and stern of a ship respectively, thus recalling those found at Palaepaphos in Cyprus and at Argos in the Peloponnese, in each case in association with tombs of warriors.[58] Both tombs there also contained skewers of iron (*obeloi*). The Salamis fire-dogs are 1.10m. long and the skewers measure 1.50m. in length. Are we to attribute a religious significance to these objects or should we consider them as having been offered to the dead merely for

Plates 51, 52
Plate 53

*Salamis*

utilitarian purposes? If we accept the latter interpretation, how are we to explain the fact that in three tombs of warriors dating from the end of the eighth century the same objects with the same ship motif were found?

The climax of the discoveries in the dromos of Tomb 79 was reached when a number of ivory plaques and pieces of furniture came to light, recalling the contents of the fabulous tombs of the Egyptian Pharaohs where chairs, beds and stools were buried with the dead king. The furniture, of exquisite quality in a rare technique, was found covered by two metres of soil in the dromos. The significance of this is unique and will be discussed below in some detail, in view of the light it throws on descriptions in Aegean literature, above all the Homeric poems. All the ivories and the furniture from this tomb were piled up to one side, together with the bronzes from the first burial, and may consequently be associated with the first, and richest, burial at the end of the eighth century BC. The fact that they have been found in a fairly good condition is another indication that the interval between the first and second burials must have been short. There were three thrones or chairs in this tomb;[59] the best preserved, made of wood now completely decayed, was completely covered with thin ivory plaques. Its seat, rectangular in shape, must have been of wood or leather straps, but nothing remained beyond a black stain on the soil. It is evident, however, that there must have been a cushion on it; indeed, traces of one were found in the vicinity of the throne, lying on the floor of the dromos. The legs and arms were thick and rectangular, but the arms and stretcher were made of thinner pieces of wood. The ivory plaques had been pegged on to all four sides of the wooden pieces. The throne has now been reconstructed and the ivory plaques have been affixed to a wooden model, which was made after careful calculations of the original dimensions. The total height of the throne is 90cm.; the height of the front legs up to the arms 70cm.; the length of the slightly concave arms 48cm.; the seat measures 50cm. × 59cm., and this is also the size of the stretcher. The thickness of the wood of the legs and arms is *c.* 6cm. × 5cm. and of the thinner pieces (stretcher) *c.* 3cm. × 6cm. The back-rest

Plate 42

Plate VI
Plates IV, V

is slightly curved and was lined inside with eleven bands of ivory, 23cm. long and 3.5cm. wide. Each was made up of a plain band on which another, carved with a guilloche pattern in two vertical rows and flanked on either side by two thin straps, was applied. Some of the carved bands remained *in situ*, others had become detached from the plain bands underneath, or had disappeared. On the lower part of the back-rest, near the seat, there are two horizontal friezes of anthemia, flanked by vertically grooved straps and separated from each other by a plain plaque. They occupy the whole width of the back-rest and are applied to (not carved on) a plain plaque, like the guilloche pattern above them. The upper part of the back-rest had a broad ivory plaque, convex on top, covered with a very thin sheet of gold, on which one may still see embossed scale-patterns. Of this, however, only few traces survive.

The second throne is of a different construction. It was made of wood, which was covered with plaques of silver, and probably also with ivory inlaid with blue glass or paste. The wood has decayed completely and the thin sheets of silver have left only traces of their oxidation on the soil; there were long narrow silver plaques on the back-rest, and the seat was decorated with similar plaques as well as six rings of the same material, symmetrically arranged. Gilded silver buttons had decorated at least the front side of the stretcher. The height of this throne was 75cm. and its seat measured 58cm. × 40cm.

Near this throne, on the floor of the dromos, there were ivory plaques inlaid with blue glass. Whether these formed part of the throne (ivory and silver sheets fixed alternately on the wood) is not easy to determine.

Next to the second throne there was a stool, also decorated with thin silver sheets. It measures 21cm. in height, and its seat 24cm. × 19cm. Its legs terminate in animal hoofs.[60]

Of the third throne very little was preserved. It was made of wood and ornamented with ivory plaques and small ivory discs, arranged in vertical and horizontal rows. Some of them were found *in situ*, but most of them had fallen off, probably by the time of its removal to the south side of the dromos during the second burial.

*Salamis*

There is no doubt that Assyrian furniture, both actual or as represented on reliefs, offers the best parallels for the thrones from Salamis. The Assyrian palaces were often adorned with splendid furniture, as the many palace reliefs show; these are supported by epigraphic evidence, where such pieces of furniture are mentioned as spoils or as gifts to the king. The palace of Nimrud has also produced a number of original but fragmentary pieces.[61] Luxury furniture, such as thrones inlaid with ivory, gold and silver, must have been circulating in the courts of the Near East, and Salamis, being under Assyrian domination from the end of the eighth century, must have had such furniture in its palaces, either imported from a Syrian centre which specialized in it, or made locally under strong Assyrian influence. Chairs of ivory overlaid with silver and gold are mentioned in oriental documents.

It is not surprising that Homer, who knew and admired oriental works of art should be aware of the existence of such luxury furniture for it may well have found its way also to the Greek Mainland. He describes the throne of Penelope as 'a chair of ivory and silver, decorated with spirals'.[62] The guilloche decoration on the first throne from Salamis and the silver on the second clearly offer good parallels for the above description. A throne of ivory with guilloche patterns was also found at Nimrud.[63]

Large ivory bands of various sizes, both carved and plain, were found in the same pile of objects near the ivory throne. These have now been assembled after cleaning and mending and have made up into a bed. The oblique terminals of the reassembled long plain bands and the four legs have helped to establish beyond reasonable doubt the identity of the object to which these ivory pieces belonged. The bed, unfortunately, unlike the throne, did not survive in good condition, due probably to its size. It was made of wood on which the thin ivory bands were dowelled. The following measurements have been obtained after reconstruction: width 1.11m., length 1.89m., height (without bedstead) 31cm., total height with bedstead 89cm.

The reconstruction of the general frame of the bed is fairly certain, but we cannot place with certainty a number of accessories which

*The Age of Exuberance*

were found together with the larger pieces of ivory. These include a rectangular frame with sides 6cm. broad and measuring 61.5m. in width and 49cm. in height. This has been placed tentatively in the middle of the frame of the bedstead. Inside it we have put three bands of carved ivory consisting of smaller plaques. Their total length is 49cm. and their height 7–8cm. The band, which we placed above, consists of six smaller plaques forming a frieze with the six-fold seated figure of the god Heh holding a branch of a palm tree from which the *ankh* symbol is hanging.[64] The representation is carved in relief, with the kilt of the god and the palm tree branch covered with a thin sheet of gold. The second band consists of four plaques carved with stylized anthemia with interlocked stems and the flower is inlaid with small pieces of blue paste. The lower band, consisting of six smaller plaques is decorated with three pairs of opposed sphinxes, with a stylized flower between each pair.[65] The aprons and head-dresses of the sphinxes, as well as the flower, are gilded with thin sheets of gold.

Plate VII

Plate VIII

At either side of the bedstead, on the upper part of the vertical pieces of the frame are two plaques, 22cm. long, which are carved with stylized anthemia and buds inlaid with blue paste and partly covered with thin sheets of gold. They still preserve the ivory pegs with which they were affixed to the wood. In their assumed original position in a row between two bars of wood towards the upper end of the bedstead, we have placed seventeen stylized ivory flowers carved in the round and with the lower part gilded; each has an iron nail through it, obviously for attachment. The head of each nail was also gilded. Once again surmising their correct location, we have set, on the front of the bars above and below this row of flowers, two narrow friezes of hieroglyph-like designs in blue paste, found scattered on the floor of the dromos of the tomb; they are 2.5cm. and 1.5cm. wide respectively. Some of them were found in position, forming a long narrow band, and we may infer that they were inlaid on a wooden bar, in the fashion of earlier Egyptian furniture.

In the same area of the propylaeum were found more ivory objects. An S-shaped leg of a table, in solid ivory, 36.5cm. high, was

Plate 44

*Salamis*

originally thought to have belonged to the bed, but this identification cannot now be considered as the bed has its own legs. The fragility of this leg would warrant a lighter use, as for instance for a table of the kind that appears in Phoenician representations.[66] The upper part of the leg was decorated with a carved representation of a sphinx (only part of the wing survives); its lower part terminates in the paw of a feline with cavities for the claws to hold inlaid blue glass (now missing). An almost identical ivory leg was found at Nimrud.[67] There must have been at least two other legs for the table, but these were destroyed during the Roman period when a substantial part of the filling of the propylaeum in front of the stomion of the chamber was removed for the construction of a staircase.

Two ivory plaques carved on both sides in openwork may have belonged to the throne. These were probably fitted between the arms and the seat; in fact their upper and lower sides are suitably formed for inserting into wood. Being 16cm. high, they fit exactly in the space mentioned. One of them represents a winged sphinx, wearing the crowns of Upper and Lower Egypt, walking among stylized flowers, also rendered in openwork. The surface of the sphinx and the flowers are in gilt cloisonné work inlaid with blue and brown paste. Exactly the same technique was employed for the second plaque which represents a composite stylized lotus flower.

Plate V

Plate IV

Lastly, we may mention an object of massive ivory in the shape of an incense burner. Such objects are known from Cyprus and elsewhere, but always in bronze.[68] The Salamis ivory could not possibly be an incense burner because it is too fragile, but it may have served some purely decorative purpose. It consists of three superimposed rows of drooping petals surmounted by three horns inserted into a disc and ending in a volute at the top. The total height of this object is 31cm. There are two others, less well preserved, but with one and two rows of petals respectively.

Plate 43

Finally, our account of the ivories from Tomb 79 should include an iron knife with an ivory handle terminating in the paw of a feline. The total length of the knife is 36.5 cm.

Plate 47

## The Age of Exuberance

Large numbers of vases of various forms and sizes were found in the dromos of the tomb. Bowls and dishes of various sizes predominate; they lay on the floor, some containing bones of chickens, some egg-shells and others fish-bones. There were also medium-sized jars like those found in Tomb 3, as well as large amphorae 80–90cm. high, painted or plain. All the amphorae were found lying against the north and south side walls of the dromos.

Plates 54–56

Since there was not any considerable chronological difference between the two burials, the pottery in each was of a homogeneous type ranging from the end of the Cypro-Geometric III to the beginning of the Cypro-Archaic I, *i.e.* around 700 BC. The fabrics are Cypriote throughout, the painted wares being either White Painted or Bichrome. Stratigraphically, however, it was possible to distinguish between the first and second burials. The dishes of the former were all in tiny fragments, scattered on the floor of the dromos and covered with a layer of soil. The bowls and dishes of the second burial lay above.

There was a distinct class of vases, obviously belonging to the first burial, which were placed in the bronze cauldron with the griffin protomes described above. They are for the most part jugs of two types which appear mainly in Phoenician pottery, at least in their original form: firstly, jugs with a sack-shaped body and mushroom-shaped rim; secondly, those with a sharply tapering neck and a trefoil mouth. All these vases were of plain ware but their surface was tin-plated, like the vases from Tombs 2 and 47 which we have already described. No doubt the intention was to make these vessels look like their metallic (silver?) Phoenician prototypes.[69] There were about sixty such jugs in the cauldron and they must have been still shining brightly at the time of the second burial, seeing that they were collected and put aside separately from the rest.

Plate 41

Apart from food, offerings to the dead included large numbers of murex shells and other sea-shells of various shapes and sizes.

Plate 50

In one of the large amphorae, fragments of a human skull and other human skeletal remains were found. These evidently belonged to the dead of the first burial, and we may therefore assume

# Salamis

that inhumation was practised for this. There is no evidence, however, concerning the nature of the second burial.

The richness and diversity of the burial gifts found in Tomb 79 is unrivalled in Cyprus. The occupants of this tomb must have been members of the royal family of Salamis, at a time when the independent kingdoms of the island, though under Assyrian domination, could carry on their own cultural and social traditions provided they paid their tribute to the conqueror. When so much luxury could be offered as gifts to the dead king – and we must bear in mind that what we have found comes from the partly disturbed dromos of a tomb of which the chamber had been entirely looted – the wealth and the power of the kingdom of Salamis may well be imagined. This is a good omen for the excavators of the city site where the palaces of these kings must one day come to light.

At one time during the past two years one of our expert diggers from the village of Enkomi described how he entered a tomb some 50 years ago in the region of Salamis which was built of regularly worked blocks, was vaulted, and decorated all over the inside 'with flowers of all colours.' Since we regarded 1967 as the last year of the first phase of excavations at the Salamis necropolis, we decided to search for this tomb. With some difficulty and consequent delay we located it finally at the 'Koufomeron' site, on the western outskirts of the necropolis, about 500m. south-west of the large tumulus (Tomb 3). This is **Tomb 80** in our register. The chamber is built of rectangular, well carved blocks of limestone inside, but the walls and the roof are strengthened outside with rubble stones. In plan it is rectangular, measuring 2.40m. × 2.15m.; it has a vaulted roof, 1.70m. above the floor level and a floor of regular limestone slabs. The chamber was actually built within the cavity of a rock-cut tomb of an earlier period, after its roof had been broken away. The dromos, cut into the rock, is that of the previous tomb. It is very short, measuring only 1.80m. × 2.70m. The façade of the chamber, 2.65m. wide, is built with regular ashlar blocks of limestone, with a rectangular stomion which has broad bands of purple paint applied to all of its three sides. The whole of the interior surface of the chamber (side walls and ceiling) was

Plate 58

*The Age of Exuberance*

covered with a painted decoration, applied directly to the surface of the stone, but much of it had worn off owing to continuous seepage of water since the looting. The side walls were painted with rows of long-stemmed lotus flowers (alternate blossoms and buds), whereas the ceiling was covered with a net pattern consisting of diagonals and 'rosettes' at their junctions. The colours used for the decoration are blue and purplish red. The style of this painting recalls the interior décor of Egyptian sarcophagi, of which this may be an imitation. It should be recalled that during the second half of the sixth century BC (the date of this tomb, as we shall show) the island was under Egyptian domination.

Plate 57

Though the chamber of this tomb had been looted, a good many objects were found in it; these included Plain White V ware jugs and bowls, alabaster bottles, silver ear-rings, hair-rings and finger-rings, beads of gold and carnelian, a pair of silver-gilt mouth-pieces and a number of silver coins of small denominations, mainly obols, belonging to the reign of Evelthon, king of Salamis (560–525 BC). The date of the coins conforms well with that ascribed to the rest of the material from this tomb.

We have already mentioned the archaeological field work of the German scholar M. Ohnefalsch-Richter in the necropolis of Salamis towards the end of the nineteenth century. He excavated several tombs which have remained practically unpublished. We learn about his activities from the *Chroniques d'Orient* prepared by the French scholar Salomon Reinach. In the *Chroniques* for 1885 Reinach reports that in 1881 Ohnefalsch-Richter excavated a previously looted tomb situated 520m. south-west of the 'Tomb of Saint Catherine' and that above the entrance to this tomb there was a high relief representing a 'monstrous male figure'. It was in the vain search for this tomb in 1964 that we came upon another part of the necropolis, situated as Ohnefalsch-Richter had indicated, south-east of the tomb of Saint Catherine, at a site known as **'Cellarka'** (meaning cells = chambers = empty chambers of tombs). The site now takes the form of a low ridge extending from north to south, where the natural rock is hard limestone contrasting with the clayey rock found elsewhere in the necropolis. This must have

Salamis

*Fig. 28*

been particularly suitable for the rock-cut chamber tombs of the necropolis which, unlike the built tombs reserved for kings and nobles, formed the last abode of lesser folk. During the three seasons of 1964, 1965 and 1967, we excavated one hundred tombs at this site, all within an area of 1092 square metres. The vast majority had been looted because, lying very near the surface, they could easily be detected. Furthermore they were usually surrounded by a boundary wall of ashlar blocks some of which were visible on the surface of the cultivated field above them. Once, therefore, the first tomb was found it was easy to discover most of the others. Some of them, however, had escaped the looters; but even those that had not, together with the material which was lying in their dromoi, made the three-seasons' work worth while undertaking. The architecture of these tombs, the burial customs and the material found in them differs considerably from what we encountered in the built 'royal' tombs. Also the fact that the site of the cemetery at 'Cellarka' was in use from about 700 BC to the end of the fourth century meant that a much longer period was presented for the study of the evolution of burial customs and even the effects of political events on them.

The tombs are entirely carved in the rock, with one exception where the chamber is built of ashlar blocks. The chambers are rectangular, with flat or gable roofs. There are often low benches against the walls for the dead, occasionally crudely rendered in the shape of a bed with legs and cushion. The stomion is also rectangular and closed with a stone slab. The dromos, with a staircase leading down to the chamber, is narrow, almost pointed at its entrance but widening as it approaches the chamber. On the

*Plate 72*

surface of the rock there are usually boundary walls consisting of a single course of ashlar blocks, enclosing both the dromos and the roof of the chamber. The function of these walls was obviously to demarcate accurately the space allocated to each family tomb for use during subsequent burials. These were all family tombs and remained in use for centuries, the older burials being removed to make room for new ones. We have already mentioned that the hard rock was confined to a narrow strip of land in this part of the

33, 34 Tomb 79 was the richest of all the built tombs hitherto discovered in the Royal Necropolis of Salamis. The large stone which served as a roof of its chamber was visible above the surface (Plate 34), and the tomb had been looted in antiquity. In the Roman period its chamber was re-used for burials but its large dromos remained intact (Plate 33) and produced, apart from a rich harvest of objects, the remains of four vehicles. Two of these belonged to the first burial (end of the eighth century), and the other two to the second burial, which followed a few years afterwards

35, 36 Large amphorae, which obviously contained liquids, and dishes, some of them still preserving traces of food in them, were found lying on the floor of the north side of the dromos of Tomb 79, *above*. On the south side were the remains of two vehicles belonging to the first burial, which were wheeled aside to make room for the vehicles and horses of the second burial. One of them, *below*, was a quadriga, and its wooden parts left clear impressions in the soil. (*See also* Plates 45, 46)

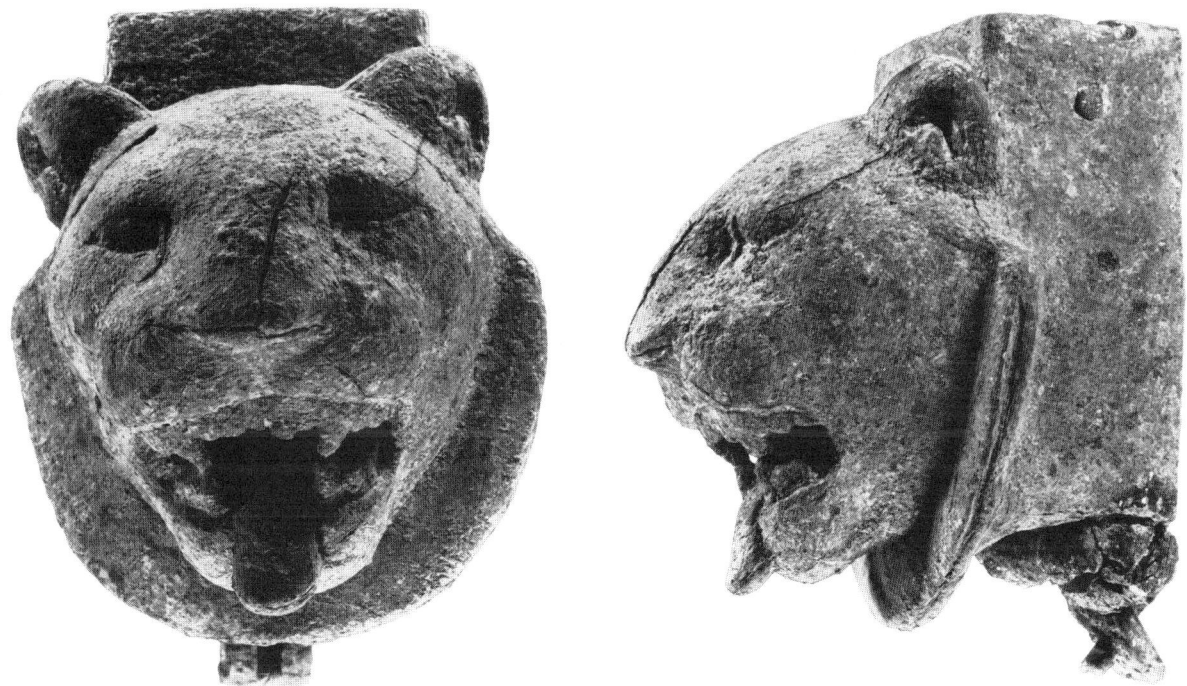

37–39 The second vehicle of the first burial found in the dromos of Tomb 79 was a hearse which had lost its wheels and its pole, but which had preserved its richly decorated body, *below*. There were five bronze heads of lions all round its floor, *above*, with hollow sockets at their top which must have contained wooden posts to support a canopy. The heads are naturalistically rendered and betray an obvious Egyptian influence

40, 41 Near the façade of the chamber of Tomb 79, on the floor of the dromos, there were two bronze cauldrons, *left*, belonging to the first burial. One of them is decorated round its rim with eight protomes of griffins and four double-faced, bearded, bird-men or sphinxes. It stands on a tripod of beaten iron rods and contained vases of plain ware, the surface of which was incrusted with tin, *below*. The other cauldron, which is very much damaged, is decorated with three small protomes of bulls below each handle, and a plaque with a Hathor's head in low relief; it stands on a high conical foot. This is the first time that cauldrons of this kind have been found in Cyprus (*see also* Plate I)

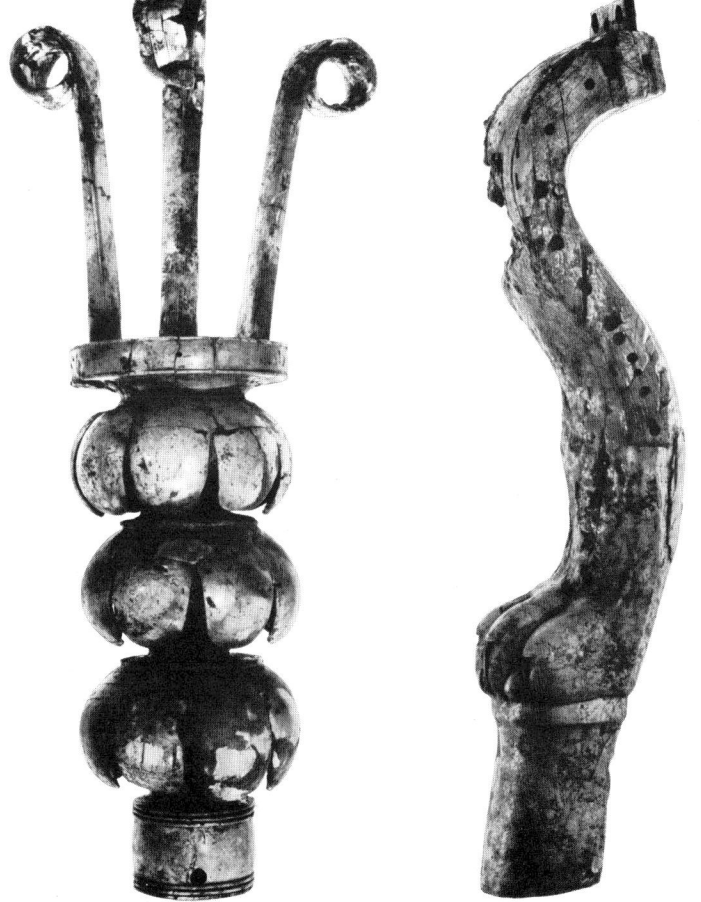

42–44 A number of pieces of ivory furniture were found in the dromos of Tomb 79 belonging to the first burial. *Above*, is a throne of wood, the whole surface of which was decorated with ivory plaques; the back-rest was decorated with bands of ivory carved with guilloche pattern and with a thin sheet of gold at the top. The wood had disintegrated completely, but the ivory plaques remained *in situ*, and the throne could be reconstructed with accuracy (*see also* Plates IV–VI). *Right*, is an 'incense-burner' in massive ivory, which imitates the shape of incense-burners in bronze; this, however, may have been solely for decorative use. *Far right*, is an S-shaped leg of a stool of massive ivory terminating in the paw of a feline, with cavities in the claws to hold a blue glass inlay. A similar ivory leg of a stool was found in Nimrud and dates also to the eighth century BC

45, 46 The quadriga of the first burial which was found on the south side of the dromos of Tomb 79 was richly decorated with metallic attachments. The terminals of the axle were decorated with bronze caps in the shape of a sphinx's head, with eyes of white paste, and a broad collar. Through the neck of the sphinx was an iron linch pin, surmounted by a bronze figurine of a fully armed soldier, cast hollow and containing a rattle inside it. The soldier wears a crested helmet and a foliated cuirass, both inlaid with paste, and holds the pommel of a sword which hangs from a belt across his chest. The total height of the linch-pin with its accessory ornaments is 56 cm., and may be the largest ever found, adding to the pomp of the ceremony both by its glitter and its sound

47–49 Among the finds from the dromos of Tomb 79 were an iron knife with a handle of ivory terminating in the paw of a feline. *Centre*, a bronze head band of a horse belonging to the first burial of Tomb 79. It consists of two pieces hinged at the middle. The upper half is decorated with a winged figure of the god El in repoussé; the lower half is similarly decorated, with a solar disc above El, and terminates in an anthemium and lotus flowers. *Right*, a bronze side pendant ornament also belonging to the first burial of Tomb 79; it is decorated with a winged nude goddess, Ishtar, in the centre, with a solar disc above her head and a number of animals all round her. She holds a lion in each hand

50 Murex shells found on the floor of the dromos of Tomb 79

51–53 A pair of iron fire-dogs from Tomb 79, terminating in the prow and stern of a ship respectively. Objects of similar form were also found in warriors' tombs at Old Paphos and at Argos in the Peloponnese, all dating to the eighth century BC. Associated with the fire-dogs were twelve iron skewers bound together with two rings in a bundle

54–56 Most of the vases found in the dromos of Tomb 79 are of Plain White ware; there are a few, however, which are decorated and help to date the two burials in the tomb to the very end of the eighth century BC and to about 700 respectively. *Right*, a hydria of White Painted ware. *Below left*, a White Painted large amphora, and *below right* a Bichrome large amphora. In the funeral of Patroklos, described by Homer in the *Iliad*, large amphorae containing honey and fat were placed against the funerary pyre

57, 58 The last built tomb to be discovered on the western outskirts of the Necropolis of Salamis was Tomb 80, dating to the second half of the sixth century BC. The stone walls of its rectangular chamber are decorated all round with stylized, long-stemmed, blue and purple lotus flowers. The ceiling of the vaulted roof is decorated with crosses and 'rosettes', or stars, of the same colours. The style of decoration recalls Egyptian prototypes. Cyprus, we know, was ruled from Egypt from 560 to 525 BC

59, 60 At the 'Cellarka' site in the Salamis Necropolis several pyres of rock-cut tombs were found near the surface. They contained small bowls, clay ornaments (rosettes, pomegranate beads), carbonized fruit, sea-shells etc., offered to the dead after the burial. *Above* is a detail of Pyre L; *below*, a group of clay rosettes, pierced twice horizontally, found on Pyre L. This is the first time in Cyprus that the custom of offering pyres with gifts to the dead had been found. It may have been brought to the island by Greek colonists at the time of their eastward expansion in the eighth and seventh centuries BC

61–63 Objects found on pyres: *far left*, a clay incense burner from Pyre A, decorated with bands of purple paint; *left*, an animal bone with a crudely engraved decoration showing a human face, also from Pyre A; *below*, a clay arm decorated with a broad bracelet round the wrist consisting of several rows of chains joined together, from Pyre AE

64 This large amphora of Bichrome IV ware is decorated round the shoulder with a frieze of lotus flowers and buds. It was found in Tomb 105 at Cellarka where there was a large quantity of this ware of the seventh century BC (*see* Plates 65–69)

65–67 Examples of pottery from the chamber and dromos of Tomb 105. *Above left*, is a Bichrome IV ware amphoriskos decorated with stylized lotus flowers. *Right*, a Red Burnished ware jug, several of which were found in the tomb, some, like those found in the griffin cauldron (Plate 40), were covered with a tin slip. *Below*, is a local Cypriote imitation of an East Greek skyphos

68, 69 Tomb 105, one of the few tombs found intact at Cellarka and also one of the largest, had its burial chamber carved out at a depth of more than three metres below ground beneath a layer of hard rock. Consequently its walls had to be built of well-dressed ashlar blocks, *below*. One of the most beautiful of the many vases found in the tomb was the large jar, *right*, from the dromos, decorated round the shoulder zone with metopes containing rosettes and guilloches

70, 71 Tomb 84 is one of the earliest at Cellarka. Though its chamber had been looted, its dromos produced pottery of the seventh century BC. It is carved in the hard rock, and preserves its boundary wall at the surface, along both sides of the dromos. The stomion has a stepped moulding on all three sides and a carved crescent in relief in the middle above

necropolis, and therefore utmost 'economy of space' was necessary in order to accommodate the dead of nearly four centuries. The early tombs (end of the eighth century) were spacious and comfortably arranged next to each other, with their dromoi turned to the east, like the built tombs, in order to face the city site. Later on, they all had their boundary walls at the top, regularly defining the space 'owned' by each particular family. Subsequently, however, when all available space on this rocky strip of land had been occupied by tombs, they began to adopt various devices in order to provide room for more burials. Very often they would dig into the sides of large dromoi in order to make small chambers. To have a separate dromos for each tomb was now regarded as a luxury and often we find chambers without a stepped dromos in front. Sometimes there is only a narrow shaft at the lower side of the stomion which opens directly into the chamber. In a few cases small chambers were carved underneath already existing ones, to create a kind of 'two-storeyed' tomb. The rock underneath the steps of the large tomb is usually carved out and in some instances only a very thin layer of rock separates the surface of the steps from the roof of the chamber underneath. Sometimes the cutting of a new tomb had to be discontinued when it was found that there was not enough space for a chamber and another one lay immediately beyond.

A number of tombs from this site, including some which have been found intact, will be discussed later. Meanwhile, we shall try to describe and interpret a phenomenon which has not before been observed in a Cypriote cemetery, namely the presence of pyres in honour of the dead situated next to the tombs or in the dromoi, about 30 or 40cm. below the surface. They usually occupy a circular hollow, 1.00m. or 1.50m. in diameter and 10–20cm. deep. These are full of ashes which are found to contain a number of offerings, namely small clay vessels, clay imitations of jewellery, sea-shells, carbonized cereals or fruit. The vases are almost always of the same types – juglets with a red slip (Red Slip III (V) ware) and small shallow bowls of plain ware. They are burnt by the fire, into which it seems they must have been thrown and obviously smashed after a libation.

Plate 59

Plates 60–63

*Salamis*

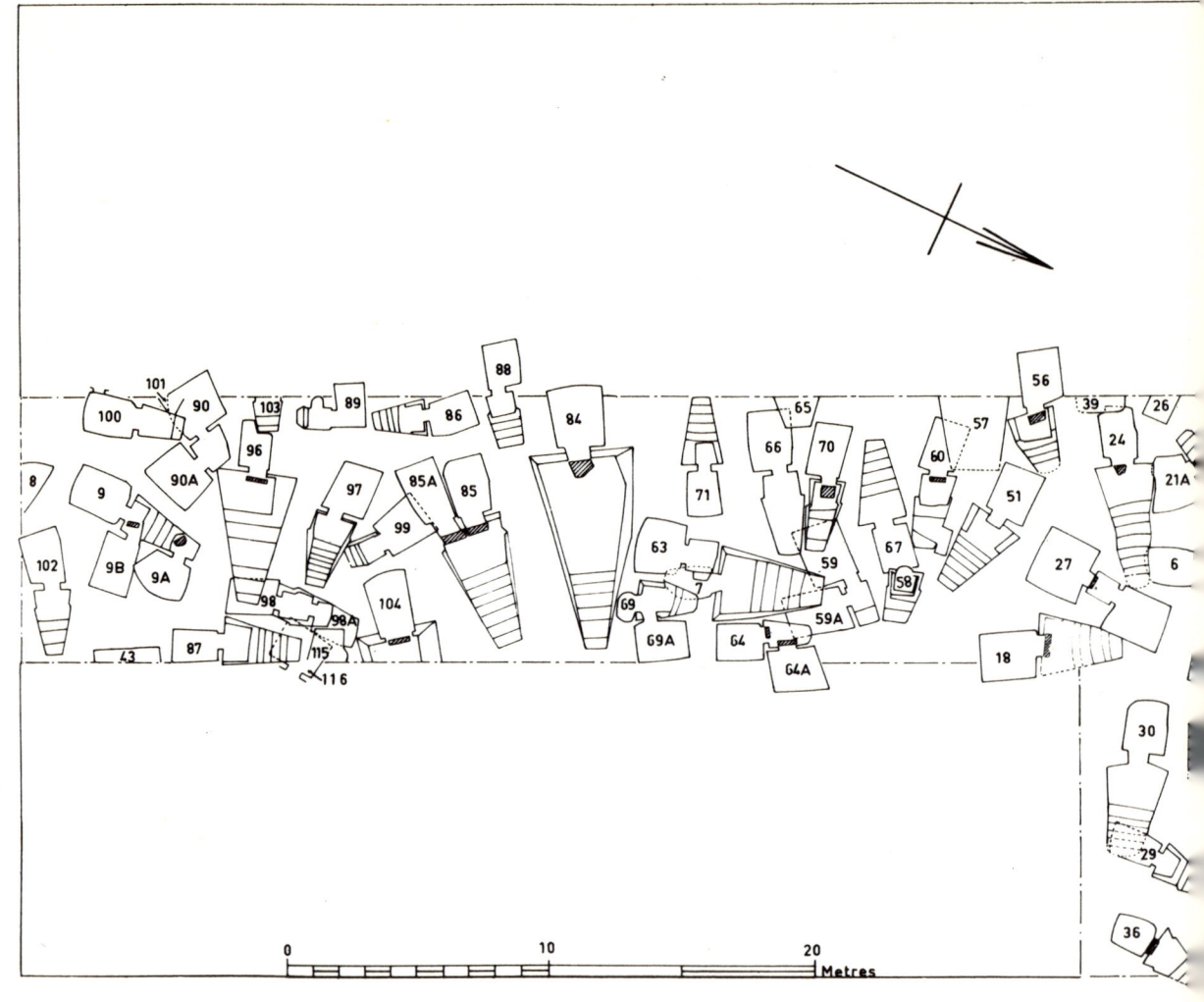

There are small stones above them and often a layer of mud covers the whole pyre.

Few of these pyres have been found intact, most of them having been disturbed when later tombs were introduced. Each seems to have belonged originally to a particular tomb, and to represent an offering by members of the family of the deceased, and subsequent to the burial, probably within a specific period after the funeral. It is certain that they have nothing to do with any

*The Age of Exuberance*

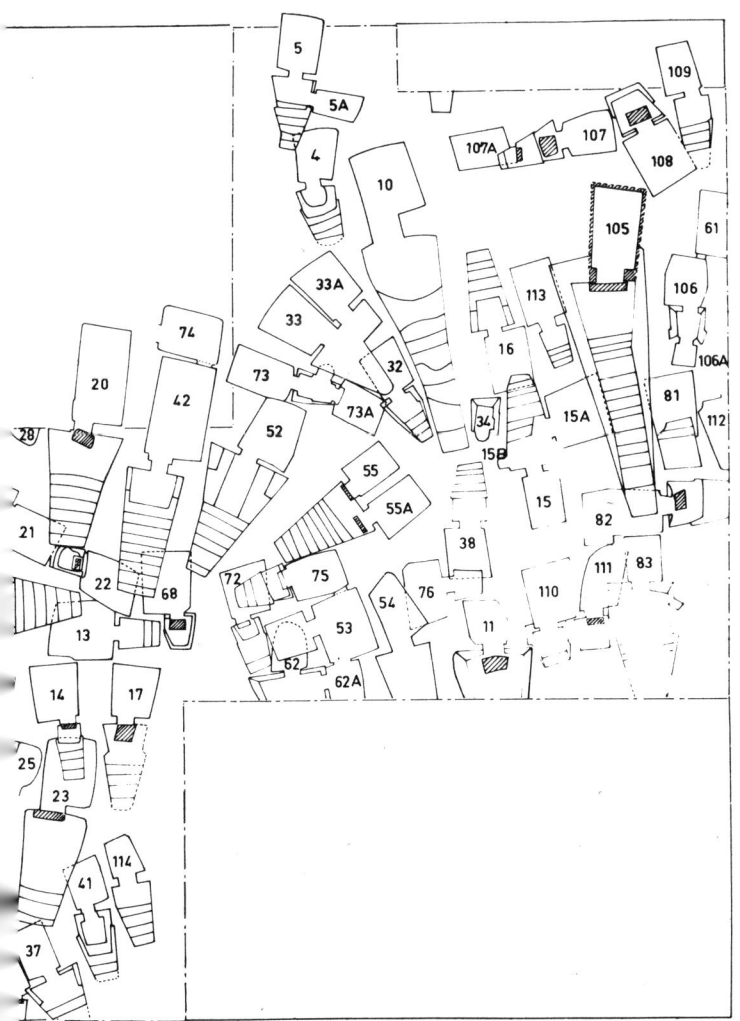

*28 Plan of the rock-cut chamber tombs at the Cellarka site of the Necropolis of Salamis showing the chambers with their stepped dromoi. The hard rock was ideal for carving chamber tombs and space was carefully utilized*

cremation, and that they are solely offering pyres. The material which they contain ranges chronologically from the sixth to the fourth century, and it seems that the practice did not pre-date the former. Such pyres, containing juglets and other small vessels are reported to have been found in a cemetery in the Athenian Agora, but those are associated by the excavators with the cremation of infants, though no traces of cremated remains have been found on them.[70] It is true that at the Salamis cemetery we have infant

# Salamis

burials, but these are always in jars or amphorae, they are inhumations and not cremations, and are quite distinct from the pyres. We are inclined to think that the Agora pyres may be offering pyres, like those of Salamis, and that this custom was introduced to Cyprus from Attica at a time when a number of Hellenic ideas (religious, political and classical) were spreading in the island as a result of political developments in Cyprus, particularly at Salamis.

We shall now describe some of the most important of these pyres. **Pyre A** is surrounded by Tombs 6, 12 and 14. It has a roughly elliptical shape, 1.00m. × 1.50m., and its perimeter is partly defined by small stones. It is in the form of a shallow basin, 10–15cm. deep, with the bottom on the bedrock. It contained ashes, charcoal and a variety of mainly small objects all bearing distinct traces of fire; the walls of the shallow cavity as well as the small stones all round it were also burnt. Mixed with the ashes and the charcoal were the offerings, about 85 in number, all of clay; they were covered with a layer of small stones. The offerings include small Bichrome V ware amphoriskoi and small jars, juglets of Red Slip ware and shallow plain-ware bowls dating the pyre to the sixth century BC; two incense burners with obvious traces of burning, which must have been used for the ritual; stemmed rosettes and perforated 'horns', decorated with a rosette, of small dimensions (5–10cm.); about forty biconical beads and a pendant, making a necklace; about a dozen small pomegranates, perforated vertically; a snake obviously associated with the chthonic gods; oblong animal bones with crudely carved facial characteristics on the one end, the hair, eyes and mouth. Such objects have been found in cemeteries elsewhere in the Near East.[71]

**Pyre L** is surrounded by Tombs 20, 21, 24 and 26; it measures 1.00m. × 55cm. and is 10cm. deep. Its contents did not differ in general from those in Pyre A. Of special interest among the ninety objects which it contained is a necklace of 32 small clay beads in the shape of pomegranates, about 30 clay rosettes (6–8cm. in diameter) also perforated, clay 'horns', small shallow bowls, juglets and jars.

**Pyre Q** was found near the surface filling of the dromos of Tomb 34 and is surrounded by Tombs 15, 16 and 32. It now measures

*The Age of Exuberance*

about 80cm. × 50cm. but must have been much larger originally. Its contents had been piled up to one side when the dromos of Tomb 34 was cleared for a second burial. The depth of the pyre is 30cm. Apart from the usual kind of pottery, it contained sea-shells, egg-shells, a terracotta figurine of a horse and rider, a terracotta of a bearded human figure, and a large number of carbonized seeds of grapes, entire grapes and almonds.

The dishes and other small vessels found on the pyres may have contained the fruit and seeds which were offered in honour of the dead. This is a custom which is connected with funerary ritual and is known also in Greek religion by the name of *pankarpia* or *panspermia*.[72] It survives in the modern Greek Orthodox religion in the practice of offering *kollyva* on the tomb of the deceased and in church on fixed days after the funeral. These *kollyva* contain boiled corn, raisins and pomegranate seeds. The clay 'jewellery' is of course a substitute for the real jewellery. It is sometimes represented 'worn' on clay hands and arms (in the form of richly ornamented bracelets and finger-rings). The eggs, the snake and the pomegranates are known to be symbols connected with the chthonic deities, but we shall not enter here into a detailed analysis of the significance of each symbol; this will be dealt with in specialist studies. What needs stressing is the importance of the discovery of the pyres – for the first time in Cyprus; indeed, they are altogether very rare. The excavation of a cemetery is normally confined to the chambers of tombs and occasionally the dromoi, but the rest of the area, outside the tombs, is rarely examined. The present discovery should, therefore, prove quite instructive where the methods to be adopted in future excavations of such tombs are concerned.

**Tomb 105**, excavated in 1967, is the largest so far of all the tombs found at the 'Cellarka' site, and one of the earliest in this part of the necropolis. It consists of a large dromos oriented east-west with the chamber to the west, like the built tombs already described. A boundary wall of ashlar blocks in one single course on the surface of the rock defines the shape and the size of the tomb which it encloses. This wall, however, was disturbed and partly removed

Plate 63

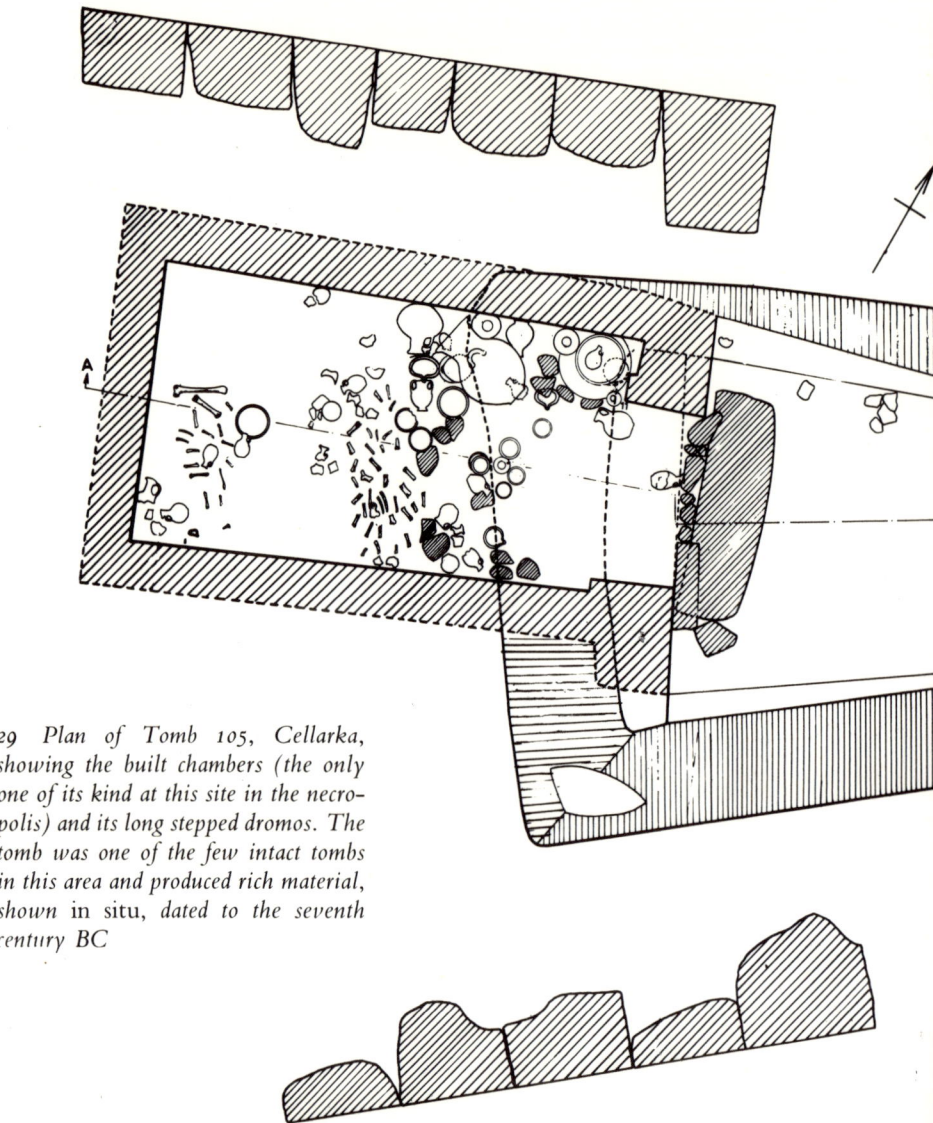

*29 Plan of Tomb 105, Cellarka, showing the built chambers (the only one of its kind at this site in the necropolis) and its long stepped dromos. The tomb was one of the few intact tombs in this area and produced rich material, shown* in situ, *dated to the seventh century BC*

at a later period when other tombs were cut in the rock all round Tomb 105.

The dromos of the tomb, entirely carved into the rock, is almost triangular in shape, measuring 9.85m. in length, 90cm. in width at its entrance and 3.30m. at the façade of the chamber. Fourteen steps lead down to the stomion. In front of this there is a small 'propylaeum', 2m. long. The first ten steps are cut in the rock and the remaining four are built or covered in a hard layer of sand and

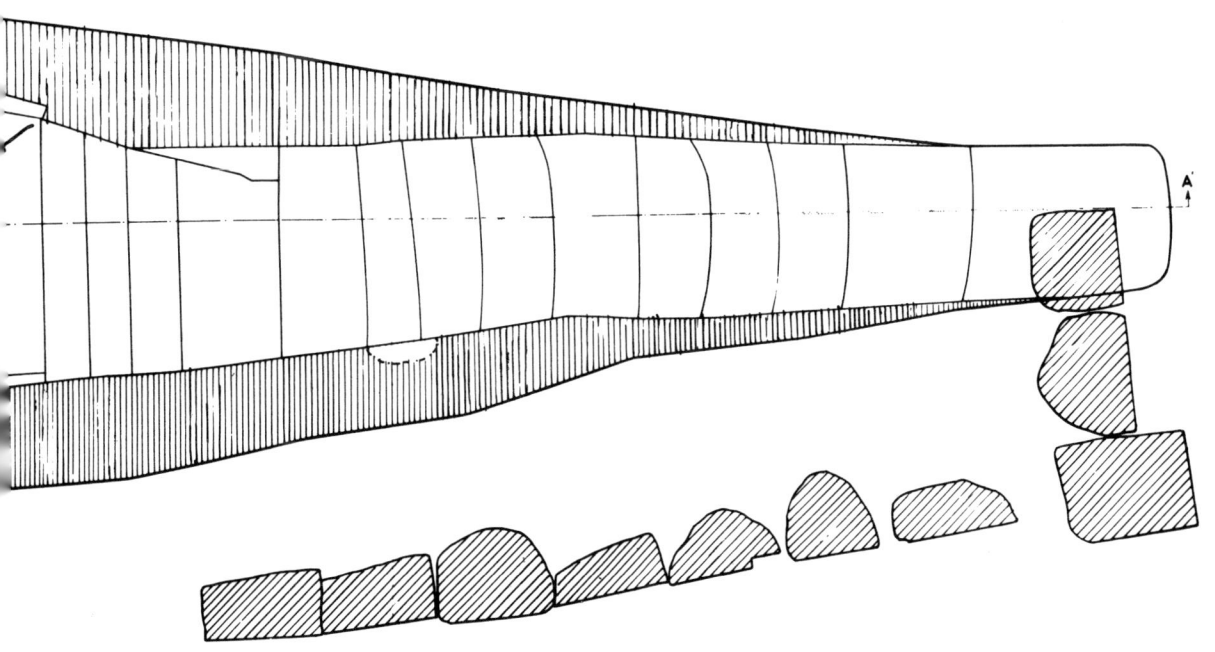

conglomerate which was found below the three-metre level in the thickness of the rock. The total depth of the tomb in front of the façade of the chamber is in fact four metres but the hard rock itself disappears below three metres. It is below this thick layer of hard rock that the chamber was constructed, but since there was only sand and conglomerate it was necessary to build the sides of the chamber with regular ashlar blocks of soft white limestone. The bottom of the layer of hard rock formed the flat roof of the

Plate 69

*Salamis*

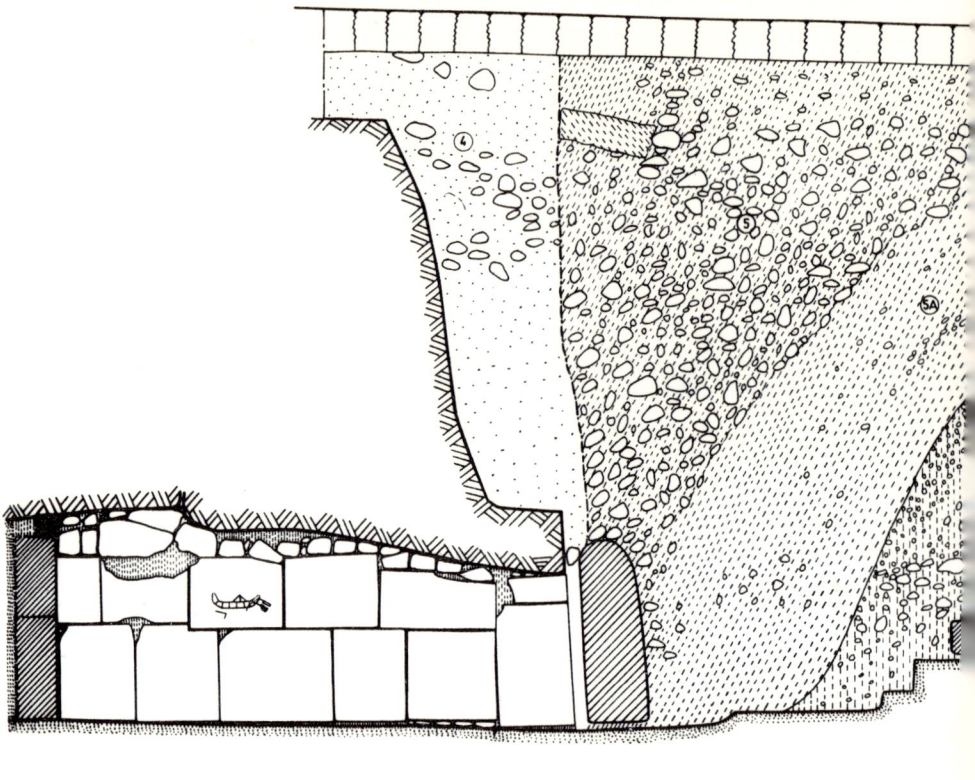

SECTION A-A

chamber. In the joints between the built sides of the chamber and the rock there was gypsum of a kind which was encountered in the construction of the other built tombs in the Salamis necropolis, *i.e.* it is ground, not baked. The regular ashlar blocks of stones, with a patina on their surface, do not seem to have been cut for this purpose but to have been taken from other ruined buildings. One of them has engraved upon it a graffito of a ship with oars and mast.

The entrance to the chamber, 1.00m. high and 1.05m. wide, was also constructed of ashlar blocks. It was closed with a large slab fixed with smaller stones all round it. The maximum height of the chamber itself, which measured 2.95m. in length and 1.60m. in width, was 1.40m. Its floor was covered with a thin layer of crushed limestone.

*The Age of Exuberance*

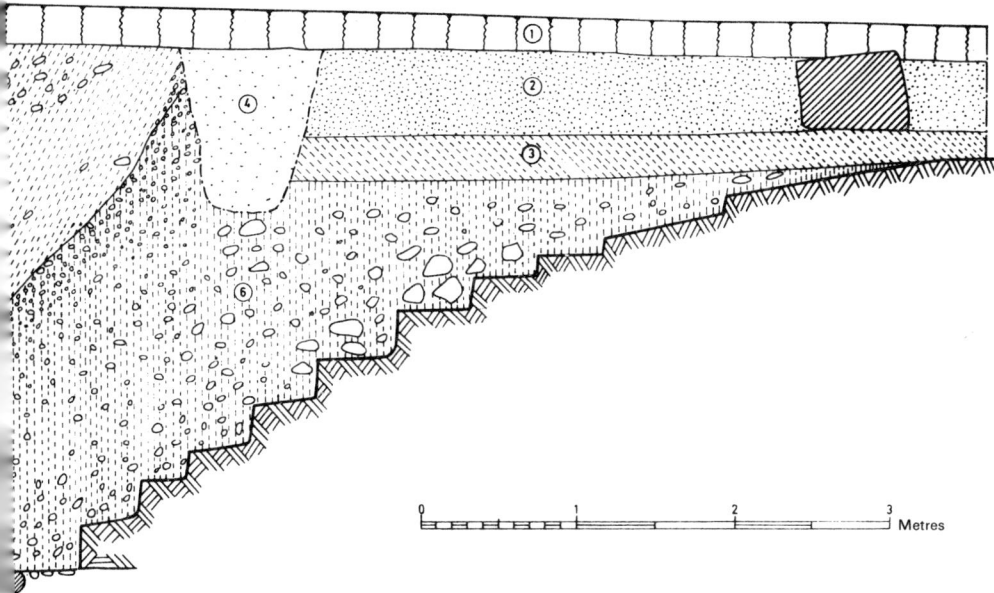

*30 Section of Tomb 105, Cellarka, showing the ashlar block construction of the chamber and the filling of its long dromos. The stratification of the latter shows the two layers representing two distinct burial periods and a looter's pit just above the entrance of the chamber*

The dromos was filled entirely with layers of soil and rubble. From a study of the stratification, it was evident that there were two burial periods in the tomb, and the material found in the chamber shows that the burials must have followed one another in quick succession. Examination of a section in the filling of the dromos shows clearly the attempt by looters to enter the tomb. In fact they did so by removing the smaller stones from all round the slab which closed the entrance. The menacing depth of the loose filling of the dromos above them or some other emergency prevented them from robbing the tomb completely, though they disturbed the bones of the skeletons, obviously searching for jewellery. Large quantities of vases were found intact in the chamber, some of them of very good quality. These included amphorae of large and medium size painted in the Bichrome IV technique

*Salamis*

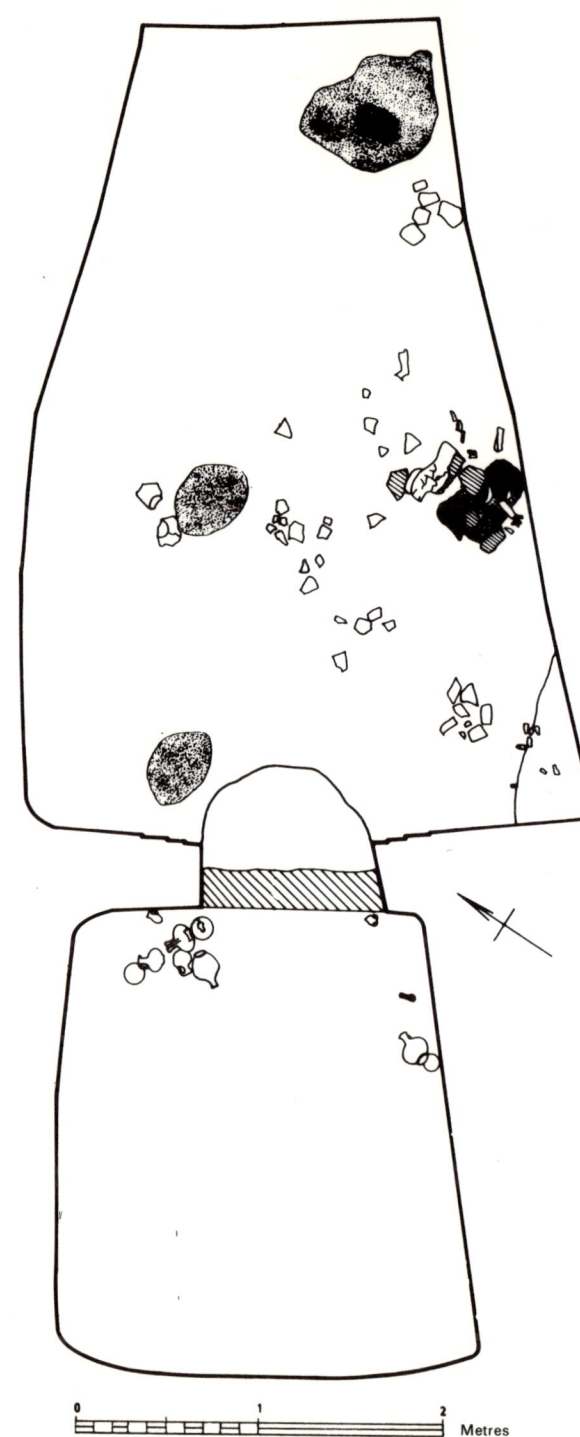

31 Plan of Tomb 84, Cellarka, showing the rectangular chamber, with objects in situ, and the rather short and wide dromos, on the floor of which traces of a large pyre were found containing burnt animal bones, evidently the remnants of a sacrifice

## The Age of Exuberance

(700–600 BC) and decorated with friezes of lotus flowers round the shoulder, as well as a number of Red Slip II (IV) juglets of the same period with a sack-shaped body and a mushroom-shaped rim, a type of vessel already encountered amongst the pottery contained in the large cauldron found in the dromos of Tomb 79 (see p. 97). Furthermore, these juglets had traces of a layer of tin on their surface, just like those of Tombs 79, 47 and 2. Also worthy of mention is a painted skyphos of local manufacture but of East Greek inspiration, of a kind which is widely known in Cyprus and Al Mina[73] and which may be connected with the appearance of Greek colonists in the East at this period.

Plates 64, 65
Plate 66

Plate 67

The dromos of the tomb also produced a small quantity of pottery, obviously removed from the chamber at the time of the second burial. Of particular interest is a Bichrome IV jar with lid, both richly decorated with rosettes and linear motifs.

Plate 68

Though this tomb is unusually large, the style of its architecture does not differ from that of the standard type of Cellarka, except for the built chamber. Considering its size and the good quality of its pottery it seems likely that this was the tomb of a wealthy Salaminian, but not of such rank as to entitle him to a burial in the 'royal' part of the cemetery.

**Tomb 84**, likewise excavated in 1967, is one of the early tombs at Cellarka, with an east-west orientation. Part of its boundary wall is still preserved on the surface. The whole of it is carved in the hard rock, but it is smaller than Tomb 105. Its dromos has a length of 7.50m. and maximum width of 4.10m., its chamber measures 2.50m. × 2.10m. It has, however, some interesting constructional features. The entrance to the chamber, 1.10m. high and 1.00m. wide, has a stepped moulding round it on all three sides and in the centre above there is a crescent carved in relief on the rock. The dromos has only seven small steps which lead to an unusually large propylaeum in front of the stomion, measuring 4m. in length and 3m. in maximum width (the width of the façade of the chamber). All over this flat surface there were very distinct traces of fire, with a layer of ashes and charcoal containing partly incinerated remains of a large quadruped which has been tentatively identified as an

Fig. 31

Plate 70
Plate 71

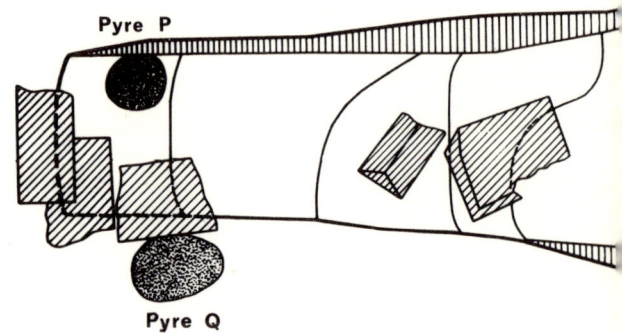

*32 Plan of Tomb 10, Cellarka, showing the rectangular chamber with objects in situ, and the long stepped dromos. Near the top of the filling of the dromos there was a jar containing an infant burial*

Plate 82

ox. This is the first time that such a custom has been observed at Salamis. We know, however, that oxen were offered to the dead and the skeleton of such an animal was found in the dromos of a tomb excavated in 1967 at Soloi near the northern coast of Cyprus.[74]

The chamber had been looted, but the filling of the dromos was intact. It contained two painted, seventh century BC Attic amphorae of the type known as 'SOS' and of which several fragments have been found in a large number of tombs at Cellarka, some inscribed in an early form of the Greek alphabet. One of these two amphorae was used for an infant burial. The same dromos also produced a plain-ware Rhodian amphora, and this too contained an infant burial.

**Tomb 10,** excavated in 1964, is one of the largest tombs at Cellarka. Its dromos is some 8m. long and its maximum width at the façade of the chamber about 3m. The rectangular chamber (2.50m. × 2.15m.) has its stomion to one side. The steps of the dromos were rather crudely cut in the rock, but the chamber inside

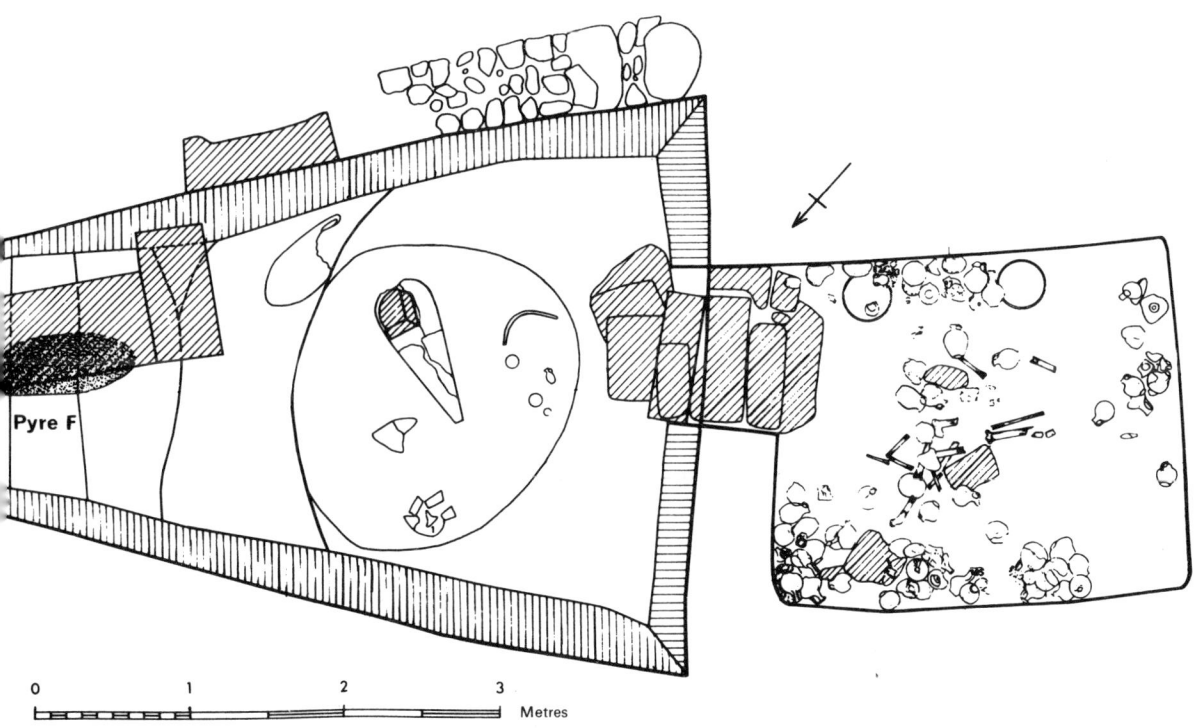

had its walls and roof plastered. Examination of the stratification of the filling of the dromos has shown that at least three burial periods were represented in this tomb; hence the 15 skulls found in its looted chamber. The first burial was connected with a horse sacrifice but the animal's skeletal remains had been piled up together with large quantities of pottery at the time of the second burial. The pottery dates this first burial to *c.* 700 BC, a date which recalls the horse burials of the built tombs of the necropolis. It included vases of Bichrome IV ware, some of them decorated with lotus flowers, as well as terracotta figurines of horses and riders, and a bull's mask. The presence of an early Attic amphora of 'SOS' type, engraved with the name of its owner(?) ΦΡΑΣΙΣ,[75] suggests that this was the ample tomb of a well-to-do citizen whose family placed the skeleton of a horse as an offering in his grave, as was the burial custom for royalty and nobility of that period. Remains of the skeleton of a horse were also found in Tomb 23 at Cellarka, as we shall see below.

*Fig. 32*

*Salamis*

*Fig. 33*

Plate X

Plate 83

**Tomb 23**, excavated in 1964, resembles in its architecture Tomb 84 described above. It is of medium size, but has in the dromos a large propylaeum measuring 3m. × 2.25m. in front of the stomion. The dromos itself, about 4m. long, had only four steps. In the propylaeum, right on the bedrock, were the disturbed skeletal remains of a horse. In a corner of the propylaeum there was a large pile of pottery, obviously belonging to the first burial in the tomb and taken out subsequently to make room for a second burial. Of particular interest is a stemmed bowl, decorated with lotus flowers in the polychrome technique. The stem itself has four standing draped female figures in relief all round it. Inside the chamber the last two burials (two skeletons) were found *in situ*. All round them were traces of decayed wood, and it is to be assumed that the skeletons were either lying on a wooden couch – there were six cavities in the floor, at regular intervals for the legs – or in a coffin. In other tombs (*e.g.* Tomb 20) we have 'couches' cut out of the rock, with even the pillow reproduced. This tomb has produced a number of painted vases of very good quality, the most important being two skyphoi decorated with meanders in the fashion of Greek Geometric pottery. In the chamber there were also large shallow bowls which contained remains of fish, evidently food for the dead. On some of the bones of the human skeletons traces of cotton (?) cloth have been found, still preserving its white and purple colour.

In the propylaeum in front of the stomion there was a pile of animal bones, apparently belonging to a horse, sacrificed in honour of the dead as in Tomb 10 described above. This is associated with the first burial in the tomb.

The tombs described above, though representative of the architecture and burial customs of the early period (eighth to seventh centuries), do not exhaust or diminish the interest of the other tombs. Indeed some of them present unique features in their architecture, burial customs etc., as for instance the occurrence of stelae on top of some of the chambers, usually in the shape of a rectangular podium; on one such podium, about 1.50 metres square and about 30cm. high, there must have stood plain rectangular stone slabs which showed above the surface; in Tomb 83, excavated in 1967,

*The Age of Exuberance*

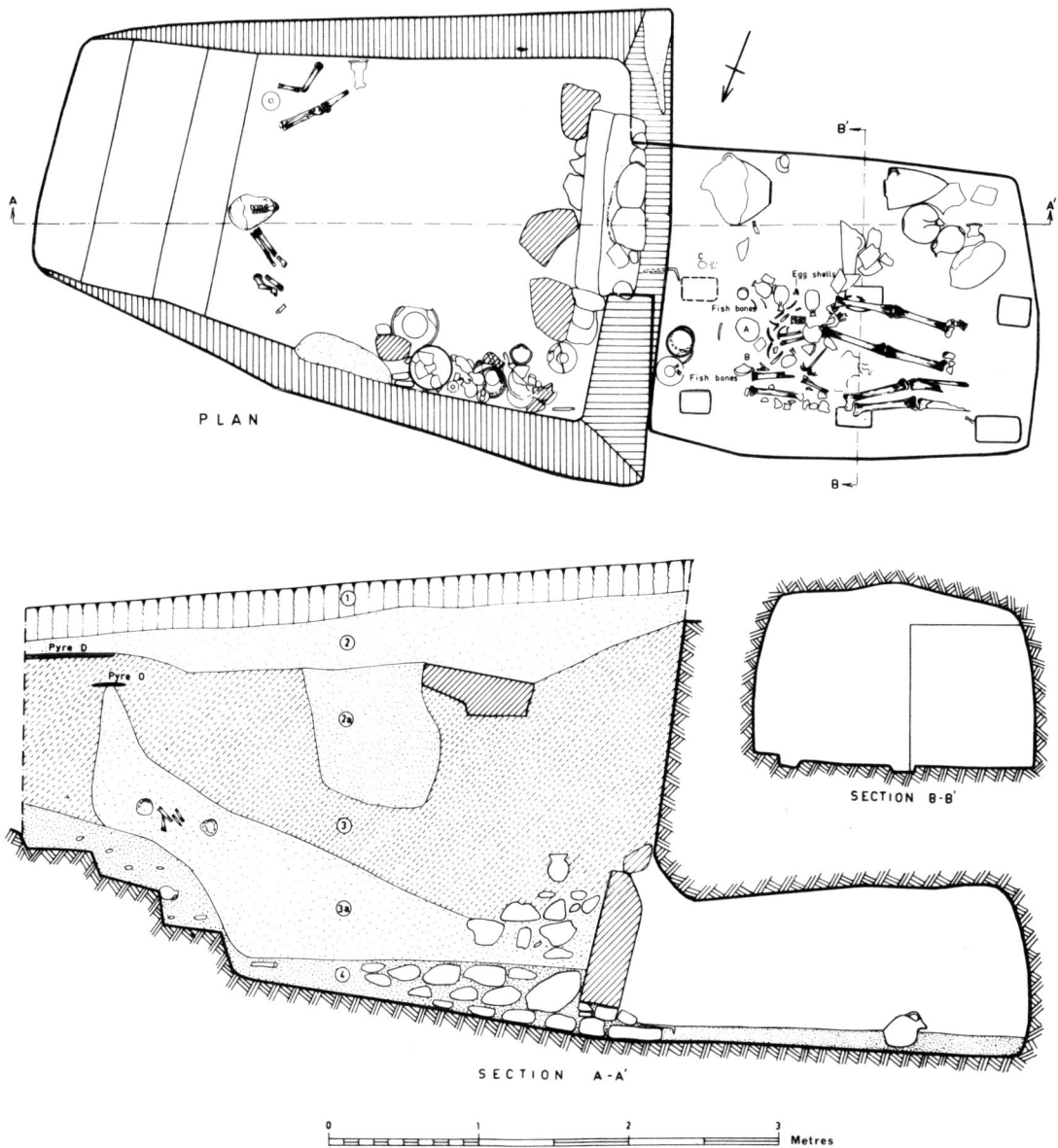

33 *Plan and section of Tomb 23, Cellarka. The plan shows (a) objects and human skeletal remains in the chamber, and (b) objects in a pile near the entrance to the chamber and the skeletal remains of a horse near the steps of the dromos. The various layers in the filling of the dromos indicate that the tomb was re-used for burials a number of times*

## Salamis

Plates 74–78, 81

Plates 82, 84

Plate 80

a human skeleton was found in the filling of the dromos, not as an independent burial, but associated with the filling of the original burial in the tomb – obviously a servant who was buried at the time as the master in the chamber. This, of course, recalls the custom of servant burials already described in connection with 'royal' Tomb 2. The pottery and clay figurines from some of the tombs which are not described here individually is of exquisite quality. Of particular importance is the occurrence of East Greek, Rhodian and Attic pottery for it illustrates the political history of this period at Salamis and indeed in the whole of the Eastern Mediterranean.

The tombs with burials dating from the end of the sixth and fifth centuries were smaller than those described above, except where they were originally made for earlier (eighth or seventh century) burials. The dromoi are narrow and short, and in some cases are absent altogether. Occasionally there is one common dromos for two or three chambers.

Their contents are poor: plain-ware jugs and bowls and alabastra (bottles) of Cypriote alabaster or gypsum. There are rarely any pieces of jewellery, even in intact tombs. Tomb 73 alone produced some gold and silver jewellery, including a finger-ring with a carnelian bezel engraved with a winged flying Eros holding a lyre and a wreath of exceptional beauty.

Some of the tombs of the classical period contained an impressive number of skeletons. Tombs 21 and 21A, with a common dromos for two chambers, contained four and ten skeletons respectively, including those of infants. In Tomb 55 there were twelve skulls haphazardly distributed, and fourteen in Tomb 59. It is interesting to note that the burial gifts were few and poor, mainly plain-ware jugs and alabastra, with very crudely painted amphoriskoi. The chamber of Tomb 113 looked like an ossuary when it was opened, with six complete skulls, many fragmentary, and piles of bones all over the floor.

It is tempting to associate the tombs of the sixth and fifth centuries with the historical events of this period, which coincides with the Persian domination over Cyprus. We have literary evidence of the resistance of the Cypriots against the Persians, their revolt

72 Tomb 6 at Cellarka. It is entirely cut in the hard rock, with steps leading down to the entrance of the chamber. At the top, near the surface and within the boundary wall, there is a large jar with a burial of an infant inside it, a custom which is not known anywhere else in Cyprus. It may have been introduced to the island by Greek colonists, as was the custom of offering objects on a pyre in honour of the dead

73 Tomb 7 at the beginning of the excavation. Large jars appear already near the surface, containing infant burials; their upper opening is usually covered with stones or with a large bowl

74–76 A number of tombs produced small terracotta figurines (*c.* 10–12 cm. in height) representing animals. They are usually painted with stripes of purple and black paint. The dog, *opposite*, horse and rider, *above*, and bird, *right*, figurines were all found in Tomb 27A

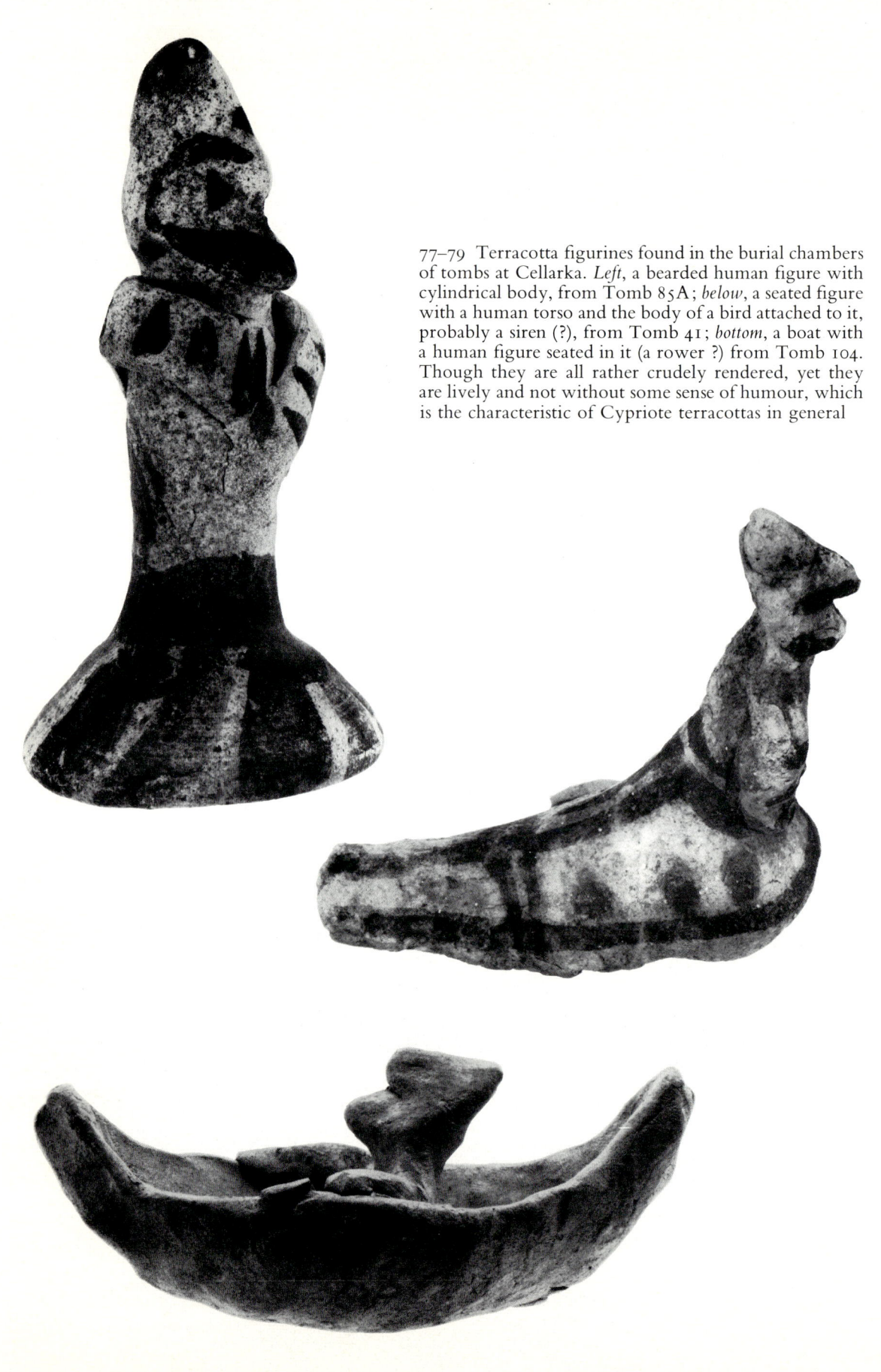

77–79 Terracotta figurines found in the burial chambers of tombs at Cellarka. *Left*, a bearded human figure with cylindrical body, from Tomb 85A; *below*, a seated figure with a human torso and the body of a bird attached to it, probably a siren (?), from Tomb 41; *bottom*, a boat with a human figure seated in it (a rower?) from Tomb 104. Though they are all rather crudely rendered, yet they are lively and not without some sense of humour, which is the characteristic of Cypriote terracottas in general

80 Ring-stone of carnelian, attached to a silver loop, from Tomb 73. The bezel shows a winged Eros holding a lyre in his right hand and a wreath in his left hand, flying to left and looking back. This is a fine gem, the work of an engraver under strong Greek influence. Fifth century BC

81 Clay model of a round shield, with its omphalos in the form of a lion's head, from Tomb 13. The shield is decorated with blue and yellow paint. Similar shields often appear in Cypriote and other Near Eastern representations

82 Large Attic amphora of the seventh century BC belonging to the so called SOS group. It was found in the dromos of Tomb 84. Such amphorae are not uncommon in the Necropolis at Cellarka and are usually associated with infant burials

83, 84 A skyphos from Tomb 23, imitating a Greek prototype of the seventh century BC not only in form but also in the decoration with maeanders, *above*. Imported Greek pottery, mainly East Greek, occurs fairly frequently in the tombs of Salamis. One of the most characteristic examples is the bird skyphos from Tomb 29, *below*, a standardized type which often appears as an import on Cyprus and other Near Eastern sites

85–87 On the south-western outskirts of the Necropolis of Salamis, near the modern village of Enkomi, rises a tumulus of earth on a rocky platform, *above*. The villagers of Enkomi first, and archaeologists afterwards, tried, through tunnelling from the top, to reach the hypothetical tomb which the tumulus covered, but without any success. In the systematic excavation of this mound which the Department of Antiquities of Cyprus undertook in 1966 the area of the tumulus was divided into segments and, starting from the top, each of the horizontal layers which formed the tumulus was removed, thus revealing the method followed for its construction. On the top of the rocky platform, but well off centre, a platform was found, constructed of mudbricks, *opposite above*. It is rectangular, measuring 17 m. in length (east-west) and 11.50 m. in width (north-south); its height is about a metre, with four steps on all four sides; the west side is broken by a ramp which gave access to the flat top of the platform. The whole structure has the look of a classical Greek edifice, and the plastered steps all round give the impression of a construction in marble. In the centre of the top of the platform a small pyramid of stones was found which covered a pyre, *opposite, below*. The fire of the pyre had blackened the mudbricks all over the top of the platform. Around the pyre were found sixteen holes, symmetrically arranged. The pyre itself contained alabastra of clay (Plate XIV), or alabaster, the former being gilded or painted; there were also carbonized almonds, figs and cereals, recalling the custom of *panspermia* or *pankarpia* of classical Greek religion, according to which the first fruit was offered to the dead. The tunnels of the looters and the archaeologists missed this platform, because they had all aimed at the central part of the mound. Those who built it possibly had the prospective looters in mind when they placed the platform off-centre, a device which has also been observed in the construction of tumuli in Asia Minor

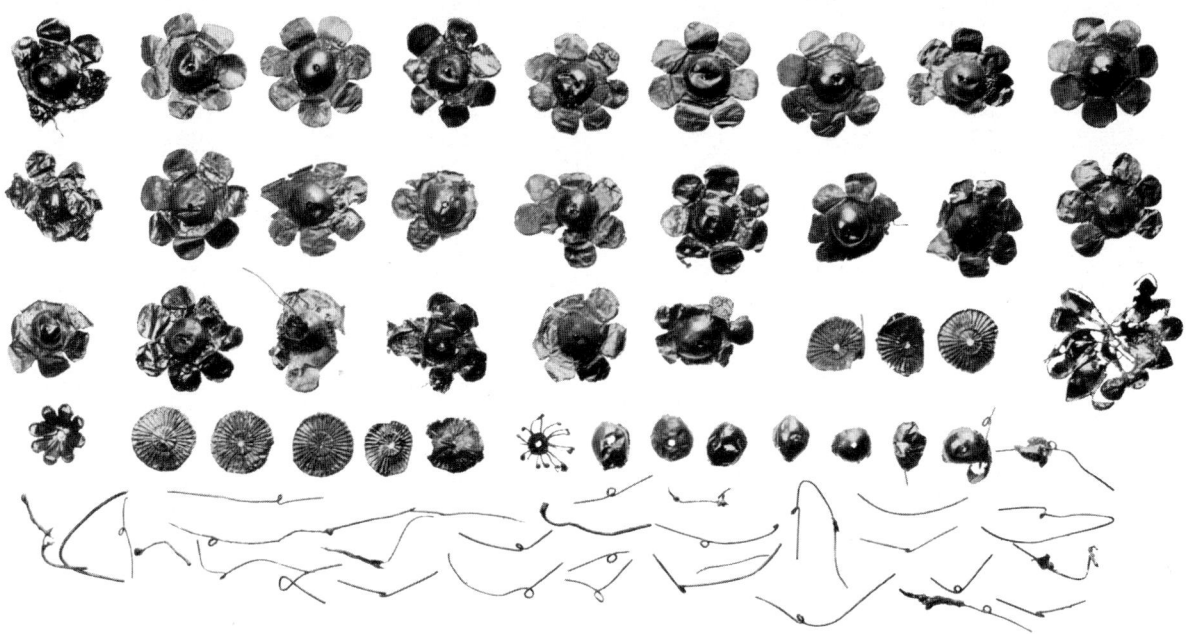

88, 89 Gold objects were found among the ashes of the pyre on the exedra. *Above* are a number of gold rosettes, evidently from a wreath. Most of the gold ornaments, however, melted in the high temperature of the fire and were collected as drops of gold. Iron spearheads were also found, *below*; right in the centre of the pyre

90–91 It was natural to expect a kind of a burial below the exedra, either a tomb or an urn containing the incinerated remains of the dead. The mudbricks of the whole thickness of the exedra were removed down to the bed-rock, *above*, without finding any traces of a burial. It was the material itself which suggested that this was the cenotaph of the last king of Salamis, Nicocreon, and his family. The sixteen holes round the pyre contained carbonized wood, *right*, evidently from wooden posts which had been erected round the pyre. These corresponded in thickness with those which had left their impressions in some of the clay sculptures found on the pyre (Plate 96)

92, 93 There was little doubt that the sculptures of unbaked clay, found in numerous fragments on the pyre, must have been erected round the pyre at the time of a funerary ceremony. Five clay heads were found, four male and one female, *opposite*. Of the male heads two were portraits of elderly figures (*above* and Plate XVI), whilst the others were of more youthful appearance, rendered rather idealistically (Plate XV), in the style of the Greek sculptor Lysippos (end of the fourth century BC)

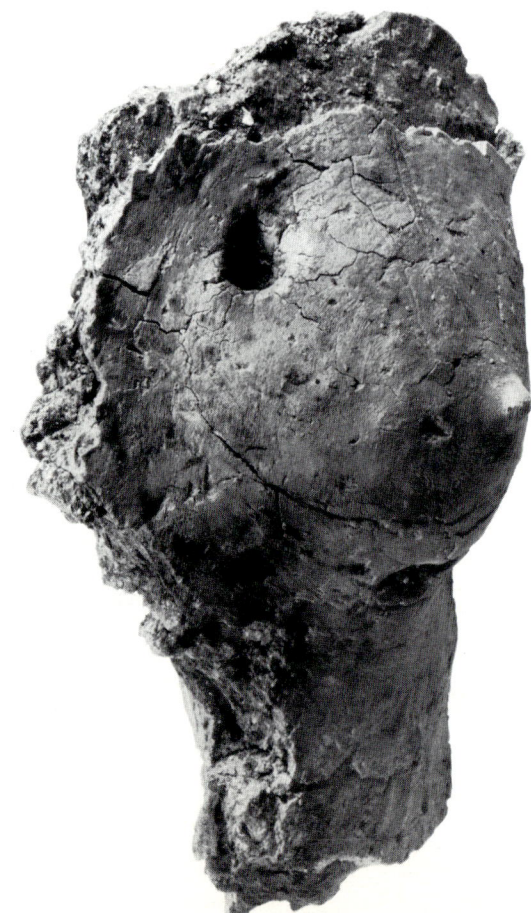

94, 95 There must have been many more than one female statue on the pyre; fragments from the chests of several female torsos were found, *right*. There was also the head of a horse, *above*, probably a substitute for a real horse, recalling the custom of horse-sacrifice in the Archaic period

96, 97 From the fragments of the statues which have been recovered it becomes clear that only those parts of the body were moulded which showed, *i.e.* heads, arms and feet, *below*; the torso was crudely rendered and was probably draped. The backs of the heads were also crudely rendered and in all cases traces of the wooden poles on which the figures were moulded, and the iron nails which had kept the clay in position showed clearly, *right*

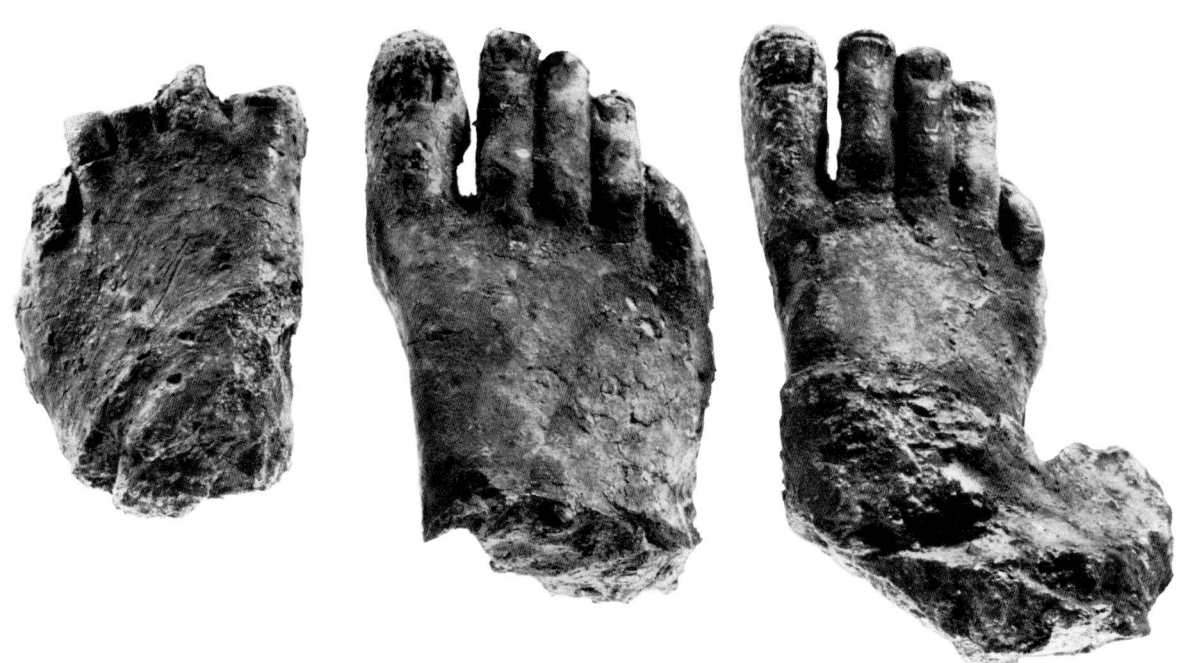

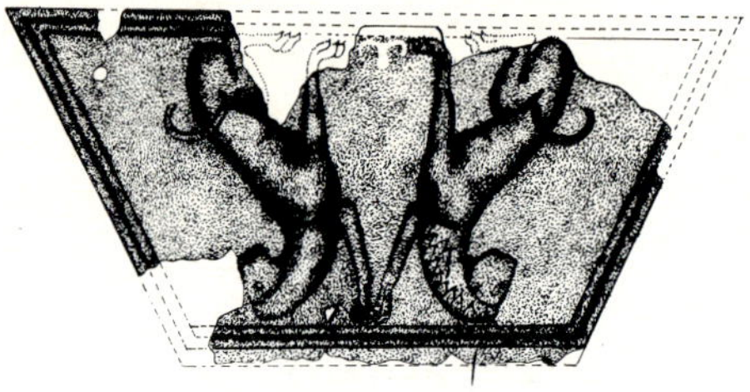

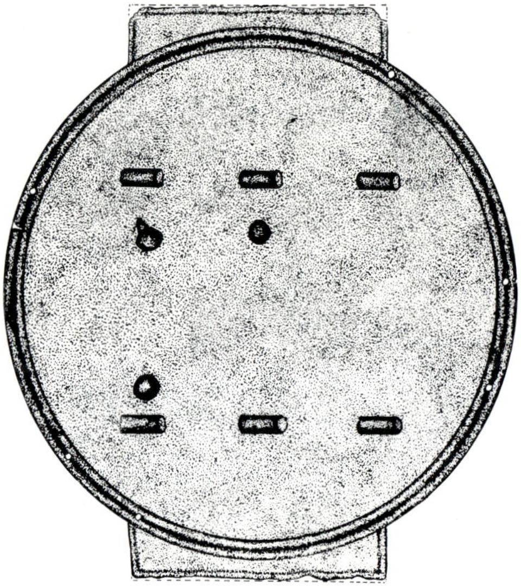

98–100 Apart from the iron spearheads found on the pyre there were several fragments of iron sheets, the armbands of shields. The main body of these shields must have been made of perishable material such as wood or leather. Some of the armbands were decorated with embossed figures of opposed lions and sphinxes, *right*, and with anthemia, *below*, recalling a style known from shields of an earlier period from Olympia

against the foreign ruler and the subsequent oppression after its failure.[76] The mass burial in small tombs with small or no dromoi, and the poor tomb gifts, may reflect the political and economic conditions in the island during this period. We know that the Phoenicians, with the support of the Persians, acquired wealth and political power and were soon to control Salamis, with the nomination of a Phoenician, Abdemon, as king of the city. The presence of the Phoenicians at Salamis is illustrated by an inscription (though in the Greek language and the Cypriote syllabary) engraved on the façade of Tomb 33 (dating from the fifth century BC), and mentioning the name of 'Abdybalos the son of Moles'.[77] Both these names are Phoenician. The language and the script of this epitaph, however, demonstrate the supremacy and persistence of the Greek Cypriote culture at Salamis, where even the Phoenicians were hellenized.

**Infant Burial.** At Cellarka we have observed a burial custom which is recorded for the first time in Cypriote archaeology, namely the burial of infants in jars. We know that this custom existed in the Aegean, as for example in Rhodes and along the Ionian coast;[78] it is interesting that there was a preference for Rhodian amphorae for such infant burials, of which more than twenty have so far been brought to light. But there were also Cypriote amphorae, with oblong body and pointed base. It is, therefore, legitimate to connect this new burial custom with the colonial expansion of the Greeks to the East, as we have already seen. Part of the amphora was broken, usually the bottom or the side, in order to make a sufficiently large hole for the infant to be placed inside; it was then put in a pit dug in the soil, or occasionally in the rock, with small stones all round it. The hole in the amphora was usually covered over after the burial with a large basin placed upside down or with a flat stone. Inside these amphorae there were usually traces of small bones, including those of skulls of infants, but in some cases, though the amphorae were intact in their pits and with the covering bowl on top, no skeletal remains were found. Clearly these must have contained newly-born infants whose bones were not yet firm enough to survive. In some amphorae small objects have been found, as for

# Salamis

Plate 72

Plate 73

example ear-rings, beads, etc. The majority of the amphorae with infant burials were found buried about 25–40cm. below the surface, usually in the filling of the dromos of a tomb or near the tomb above the roof. It is probable that dead infants were thus buried next to their family tombs. In one case, four such amphorae were found in a row, one next to the other.

The amphorae in which these infant burials were found date mainly from the end of the seventh and the sixth century BC.

Another burial custom is indicated at Cellarka, and also elsewhere in the cemetery of Salamis, by the occurrence of graves very near the surface. They consist of ditches dug in the soil about 50cm. wide, 1.50–2m. long and 25—50cm. deep, in which the corpse was buried and covered with soil. Occasionally a jug or a bowl of the early Hellenistic period was found in association with these burials, but more commonly nothing at all. Stratigraphically they belong to the latest use of the Cellarka site as a necropolis, with the pits dug into an earlier pyre or the filling of the dromos, or so as to destroy parts of the infant burials. One is tempted to associate the burials with the period of war and turmoil which persisted at Salamis during the second half of the fourth century. It is recorded that in one battle at Salamis in 306 BC some 1000 men lost their lives.[79]

The site at Cellarka, having served as a burial ground for nearly four centuries, could not accommodate more dead after the end of the fourth century and must have been abandoned for a new one, probably towards the north, where the city had already started to expand in the Hellenistic period. In fact Hellenistic tombs have been found near the village of Ayios Serghios, within the perimeter of the Salamis necropolis where the Salaminians buried their dead also during the Roman period.

The cemetery site at Cellarka has not given us anything to compare with the wealth and exuberance of the 'royal' cemetery. Yet even from its looted tombs we have collected a mass of information about new burial customs, hitherto unknown in Cyprus, which may help to clarify a period in the history of the island known only from limited literary sources.

# IV

# A King's Cenotaph

On the eastern outskirts of the village of Enkomi, on a piece of rocky and elevated ground running along the northern edge of the marshy land which was once the bed of the river Pedieos, there is an artificial tumulus of earth which belongs to the necropolis of Salamis, though at some distance from the other tombs already excavated. This particular site must have been chosen for the purpose because of its relative height, for it dominates the adjacent plain.

Plate 85

The obvious interpretation would be that this tumulus, like the other tumulus in the same cemetery which covered Tomb 3 (described above, p. 67), was built in association with a burial. Several attempts were made by looters in the past to discover a tomb underneath this challenging mound. The villagers of Enkomi, Cesnola,[80] and archaeologists of a British expedition in 1896,[81] all tried by tunnelling to reach the tomb from the top of the mound. They reached the bed rock, they even dug into it and all round it, without finding any tomb. They concluded that this tumulus, like that of Tomb 3, 'had been ransacked long ago'. Since, however, the looters from Enkomi, who are usually well informed in archaeological matters of this kind, assured us they never found a tomb under the tumulus, we were encouraged to undertake a systematic excavation of the mound, by digging the tumulus and studying its stratification and not using the unreliable method of tunnelling. The result was most rewarding; not only did we discover how the tumulus had been constructed but we were able to find out why it was built.

The tumulus, as already mentioned, consists of an artificial mound of earth which was piled on a circular platform, cut out of a rocky strip of land, measuring 52m. in diameter and 2m. in height. The

## Salamis

Plate 85

height of the mound was, when we started the excavation, 10m., but it must have been more originally, having suffered from weathering and successive tunnelling. It was built to a carefully conceived plan. The earth was piled in horizontal layers, with terrace walls of rubble and mud-bricks all round and other walls radiating from the centre; these were repeated in the form of concentric circles and radii as the height increased, at intervals of about a metre.

Thus the soil could be kept together in a pyramid, and the centre clearly defined as construction proceeded. We have seen that a similar method, though less perfected, was used for the construction of the tumulus above Tomb 3. In order to raise such a mound, soil had to be collected from every suitable place in the vicinity, and its texture and contents help to identify its source: in some layers prehistoric material, including bronze tools, was found, obviously taken from the nearby Late Bronze Age settlement of Enkomi. There were also three limestone statues, about a metre high, that had evidently belonged originally to a temple or sanctuary at Salamis. A large number of Rhodian wine jars were found as well as pottery ranging in date from the seventh to the fifth century BC which may come from another site within the necropolis of Salamis, probably Cellarka, where a number of Rhodian amphorae used for infant burials were lying near the surface. The most important of all the finds from the filling was a large bronze shield of an archaic Greek type, decorated with composite guilloche patterns all round the border. This shield, circular in shape, was found folded in two, and may have belonged to a sanctuary or tomb. The most recent material found in the filling dated to the fourth century BC and this date served at the early stages of the excavations as a convenient *terminus post quem*. Three-quarters of the soil of the mound was removed, and all the features in its construction were studied

Plates 86, XI

and recorded in plans and sections. The remaining quarter was left as a section to show the component layers of the mound and at the same time to act as a check.

On the flat surface of the circular rocky platform, somewhat south of the centre, was found a large exedra built of sun-dried

## A King's Cenotaph

mud-bricks, which the tunnels of the nineteenth-century excavators had missed. Rectangular in shape, it measures 17m. in length (east-west) and 11.50m. in width (north-south), and is about a metre high. There are four steps on all four sides, but in the middle of the western side there is a ramp leading up to the flat top of the platform. The sides of the ramp, as well as the steps, were covered with a thin layer of white plaster which gave this extremely regular and carefully built structure the aspect of a marble edifice of the classical period. In fact such edifices are known from descriptions of ancient Greek writers, and we may cite the example of the altar of Artemis Lafria at Patras, described by Pausanias.[82]

The ramp leads up through a corridor between two parallel parapet walls 2.20m. long and about a metre high. Beyond these walls, in the centre of the platform, a small mound of rubble stones was found, measuring 1.78m. in height and 5.70m. in diameter at the base. Its surface was covered with a thin layer of mud. All round this mound the clearly defined mud-bricks were blackened by fire, the traces of which covered almost the whole mud-brick surface of the top of the exedra. Small pieces of charcoal and ashes were found scattered about, as well as carbonized seeds and cereals; there were also some iron nails. Surrounding the mound of rubble, between the parapet walls and in the four corners of the platform there were rectangular holes, about 40cm. deep, symmetrically arranged. Some of them contained carbonized wood, thus explaining their original function.

Plate 91

We started with the excavation of the mound of rubble, leaving a section across the centre. Below the layer of mud and burnt rubble there was a thick stratum of mud-bricks; they had been thrown in rather carelessly, except towards the bottom where there was a horizontal layer about 50cm. above the floor of the platform. When these were removed we found a large pyre delineated by a circular boundary wall of stones. The pyre consisted of a large number of objects mixed in with a layer of ashes and large pieces of charcoal, up to a thickness of about 30–35cm., giving the impression that they had been thrown in or piled up rather carelessly. There were about one hundred alabastra bottles, of an

Plate 87

Plates XII, XIII

Plate XIV

*Salamis*

average height of 23cm., some in clay, others in Cypriote alabaster (gypsum). The clay alabastra were covered with a thick slip of white paint on which very thin sheets of gold were applied to create an over-all gilded surface. In many cases the fire had destroyed the thin gilding and only the white paint survived, in others there was paint applied on the white surface, in blue, black and red colours. Few of the alabastra of gypsum survived intact, most of them having been deformed in the high temperature of the pyre. There were also hundreds of iron nails, of an average length of 15cm., as well as several bronze rivets and attachments. There were strigils of bronze and iron, some of the iron ones having a gilt surface, and a number of iron spear-heads were found right at the bottom of the pyre. In addition, thin sheets of iron of various sizes were collected from all over it. These have now been put together and form arm-bands of shields, some plain, others decorated in repoussé with anthemia or with figured representations such as compounded sphinxes or lions. The forms of these arm-bands and their accessories, as well as their embossed decoration, bear such a close resemblance to those of the early classical period found in Olympia,[83] as to suggest that they were imported from Greece with or without the shield proper, which having almost certainly been made of leather and wood, left no traces after the fire. Round their border the shields had narrow bands of iron sheets, which have been found. These, together with the number of arm-bands, suggest that there were probably five or six shields on the pyre. Several rivets and small fittings of bronze may also belong to the shields for the attachment of leather straps at the back.

Plate 89

Plates 98–100

Other objects deserving of mention found on the pyre include remains of wreaths, namely rosettes of myrtle leaves of gold or gilded bronze, small berries of gilded paste, obviously belonging to the wreaths, small flowers (lilies?) of gilded terracotta, a terracotta pomegranate, etc. The gilded wreaths of bronze, paste and terracotta flowers, leaves and berries recall work produced in Alexandria at the very end of the fourth century. Some of them were found round the shoulders of funerary hydrias. There must have been many more rosettes and other ornaments of gold which,

Plate 88

# A King's Cenotaph

however, melted in the very high temperature of the pyre and became drops which were collected in fairly large numbers from the bottom layer of ashes.

The most important and most unusual objects found on the pyre were fragments of clay statues, some life-size and some just under life-size, which were evidently baked and hardened in the heat of the fire. They were not made of terracotta, and their uneven baking resulting from direct but intermittent contact with the fire caused cracks all over their surface. Furthermore, some of them which fell on the ground before baking were deformed and flattened. They represent human figures, except for one which is the head of a horse. Five human heads have been found. One is female, life-size, with idealized facial features, half-open mouth and impressionistic hair, recalling the style of classical Greek sculpture at the end of the fourth century. The face must have been painted white (now discoloured) and the hair was painted red. There is red paint also on the lips and eye-balls. Of the male heads two are life-size, representing young men with idealized facial characteristics, some of which recall the style of the Greek sculptor Lysippos, as for instance the half-open mouth, deep corners of the eyes, fleshy eyebrows, and impressionistic treatment of the hair. The face does not seem to have been painted – it has the pale colour of the clay used for the moulding – but the hair is painted purple. It falls on the forehead and has a centre parting in the well known fashion of Lysippos's type portrait of Alexander the Great. The other two heads are slightly smaller than life-size, and have the characteristics of portraiture. On their faces there are traces of thick red paint, but there are no signs of paint on the hair, which is in fact crudely rendered. It is possible that these two heads were crowned with wreaths and their hair was thus not meant to be seen. One of them has a well preserved face; the mouth is half-open, with the upper teeth clearly showing; it is more or less square, with rounded cheeks and a prominent chin with a dimple. There is a double-curving line for the eyebrows and the eye-balls are rendered by means of incisions. The second head is less well preserved. It was slightly deformed when it fell to the ground before baking but its general facial

Plate XII

Plate 94
Plate 93

Plate XV

Plates 92, XVI

Plate XVI

Plate 92

XI–XVI The cenotaph of Nicocreon, last king of Salamis. On a circular platform, carved out of a rocky strip of land, a rectangular exedra was built of mudbricks, on which a pyre was offered in honour of king Nicocreon and the members of the royal family who committed suicide in 311 BC (*see* Plates 85–100). Rich offerings were placed on the pyre. All round it there were the effigies of the members of the royal family in unbaked clay. At the end of the ceremony a tumulus was piled above the exedra and the pyre, covering offerings and statues. The latter, baked in the fire, were generally found in pieces but some of the heads were found almost intact (Plates XII, XIII, XV, XVI). One was a female head (Plate 93); four were of male figures, of which two were portraits, with the facial characteristics strongly accentuated (Plates XVI and 92). The other three were of young men (Plate XV), idealized in the style of the Greek sculptor Lysippos, who executed the portrait of Alexander the Great

Large numbers of alabastra (bottles) were found on the pyre of the cenotaph; some were of local alabaster, others of clay; the latter were either painted with ribbons or stripes in red and black on a white background, or they were gilded with thin sheets of gold applied on a thick slip of white paint

XI

XII

XIII

XIV

XV

XVI

XVII In one of the niches of the south sudatorium of the Baths of the Gymnasium a wall-mosaic was found, dating to the end of the third century AD, representing the River God Evrotas (his name appears in Greek capital letters above his head), reclining, with his right elbow supported on a reversed jar from which water is flowing. The god looks at Zeus (as a swan) and Leda (missing); an Eros flies above their heads. The representation, within a rectangular frame, was blocked by masonry in Early Christian times, which damaged the largest part of it (*cf.* also Plates 123, 124)

# Salamis

characteristics do not differ from those of the head just described.

Plates 95, 97

There must have been many statues apart from those to which these heads belonged. Their remains are very fragmentary, such as feet and legs of young men, in a few instances of boys, and breasts of at least two female figures. The bodies of male figures are painted pink. In most cases, however, the fragments of burnt clay which belonged to these statues do not show any trace of moulding, but appear as simple shafts with the finger-prints showing on them. This suggests that the bodies of the statues were draped and that therefore the only parts that needed moulding were those that showed, *i.e.* the face, arms, and legs. Fragments of drapery have been found, in some cases covered with thin sheets of gold. There are also fragments of several conical bases, painted red, which may have supported heads or busts.

Plate 94

The moulded head of the horse referred to above is half life-size, very naturalistically rendered, but no traces of the rest of the body have been identified.

Plate 96

There is ample evidence to show how these statues were moulded. At the back of the heads and in the 'core' of the body-shaft or within the legs were found the impressions of rectangular beams of wood and even traces of wood with iron nails still protruding from them. There is little doubt that these statues were moulded on wooden shafts studded with iron nails to hold the soft clay in place during moulding. This is the reason why so many iron nails have been found in and around the pyre. By comparing the dimensions of the wood impressions in the statue fragments with the actual

Plate 91

wood found in the sixteen holes on the floor of the exedra round the pyre, we estimate that there must have been sixteen statues mounted on wooden poles which had fitted into these holes. When the fire was lit and spread, the wooden shafts must have caught fire too, whereupon the statues fell, some still in their half-baked condition (which accounts for their deformation); others will have

Plate 93

been baked before falling, as for instance the female head.

On the pyre large numbers of seeds, cereals, and fruits were found in a carbonized condition. Of these, particular mention should be made of wheat, almonds, raisins and figs. The customs

## A King's Cenotaph

of *pankarpia* or *panspermia* have already been referred to in the discussion of the cemetery at Cellarka (p. 121). We know that figs in particular were often associated with this custom.

Having removed the objects from the pyre as well as the ashes and charcoal, we were expecting to find traces of a pit with an amphora inside it containing the cremated remains of the dead man in whose honour the pyre and the tumulus had been made. Nothing, however, was discovered on the heavily burnt surface of the mud-bricks. A section was cut across the exedra, all the four horizontal layers of mud-bricks and the soil between them being removed, until bedrock was reached throughout the extent of the exedra, except for the space covered by the steps, but no traces of a burial, whether inhumation or cremation, were found. We had to conclude therefore, that, although the tumulus and the pyre were connected with a funeral, there was no burial there – that the whole monument was constructed as a cenotaph. The perfect condition of the plaster round the steps and on the ramp of the exedra suggested that this edifice was used only once for a specific ceremony, after which the steps and the ramp were plastered and never walked upon again. This ceremony with a pyre and offerings could only be associated with a funerary ritual, particularly seeing that everything was covered by the tumulus after the ceremony. The possibility that it could have served any other function, for instance a sanctuary, must be dismissed on the evidence of the finds and the condition in which they were found. If it was indeed a cenotaph, then it follows that it must have been erected for a very important figure of the city of Salamis, probably a king. The style of the finds from the pyre, especially the Lysippan style of the clay heads, suggests a date towards the very end of the fourth century BC. Significantly, the history of Salamis during this period makes mention of an extraordinary event that took place in 311 BC, namely, the death by suicide of the last king of Salamis, Nicocreon, and all the members of the royal family.[84]

Ancient writers treat of this tragic event in detail, describing how King Nicocreon refused to surrender to Ptolemy and how he and all the members of the royal family committed suicide; Queen

Plate 90

Axiothea persuaded the king's relatives to do likewise, and finally she set fire to the palace before taking her own life. So the whole royal family of Salamis was buried under the ruins of the burnt palace. The Salaminians obviously could not easily recover the corpses from below the ruined palace for a proper burial. So, we suggest, in honour of a valiant king and his family they made a cenotaph on which they put all those objects which they would normally have put in a tomb. By offering them a pyre they thought they would expiate the souls of the dead who, having suffered a violent death, could harm the living. Round the pyre they must have erected the effigies of the dead persons. They probably possessed portraits of the king and his brothers which they could copy in clay during the short period before the funerary ceremony; of the others, the women and the princes, they probably made idealized portraits. The bodies were draped and the king and the queen were probably wearing wreaths on their heads. In this way the members of the royal family could partake, through their effigies, of the honours which the Salaminians were offering them. We are conscious that there is a certain amount of conjecture in identifying this monument with the cenotaph of King Nicocreon, but up to now this seems the only possible interpretation to place upon this archaeological material. If correct, it links us directly with one of the most noble kings of Salamis, and the last of a series of illustrious rulers.

# V

# The City Site

In the introduction reference was made to the excavations which have been carried out within the area of the city site as well as to the looting and damage which this site suffered during the last one hundred years or so. In this chapter we shall describe recent archaeological research, mainly that which has been undertaken by the Department of Antiquities of Cyprus since 1952.

We have mentioned the outstanding discoveries of the French expedition of the University of Lyon (Institut F. Courby) within the city site, where apart from a tomb of the eleventh century BC there have been brought to light a city wall of mud-bricks and houses which date from the very early years of the foundation of the city. These excavations are still in the stage of preliminary trial investigation, and it is as yet too early for full architectural discussion to be undertaken.

Plates 1–3

Salamis of the archaic and classical periods must have developed in the south sector of the ancient site, all round the harbour, though over a much wider area than that which was covered by the Early Geometric city. The latter is the area lying immediately to the east of the archaic and classical necropolis which we have already described. No major architectural remains from this period have so far been found, though the French expedition may come across them very soon at the site now being excavated near the harbour area.

There is evidence that apart from the habitations and public buildings which must have existed at the city site, there were also sanctuaries outside the boundaries of the city itself, like the rural chapels of villages in the same district, themselves lying at a distance of about 500m. from the village. Such sanctuaries were discovered late in the nineteenth century in the vicinity of Salamis and the

*Salamis*

finds, mainly terracottas dating to the sixth century (which marks the floruit of sanctuaries throughout the island), are now scattered in various museums without any record of their discovery.[85]

Plates 101–103 During recent years a number of fragmentary limestone statues, either life-size or statuettes, have been found in an area between the village of Enkomi and the Monastery of St Barnabas, west of the city site, and within the boundaries of the archaic necropolis. An excavation undertaken by the Department of Antiquities in collaboration with the French expedition of the University of Lyon revealed that these statues came from a cache, the deposit (*bothros*) of a nearby sanctuary, of which no traces have been found. The statues and statuettes found in the *bothros*, though fragmentary, are of importance because of their stylish resemblance in a number of instances to the *kore* of Greek sculpture. The statuettes, about 30–50cm. in height, represent female figures dressed in a chiton and a himation; with one hand they hold the edge of their himation, with the other a flower in front of their chest. Their shoulder-length hair falls in abundant tresses. Red colour, still preserved, was used to render the embroidered flowers and other motifs on the draperies. The style is so close to that of the end of the sixth-century BC *korai* from the Athenian Acropolis that one should accept that this type of sculpture was introduced to Salamis either indirectly through the importation of Greek originals in marble or directly

Plate 127 by Greek artists working in Cyprus. A limestone *kore* of similar type but larger was found during the excavations of the Gymnasium, showing how widely this style was known at Salamis.[86] This is not surprising if we recall that the end of the sixth century is a period of very close cultural political contacts with the Greek Mainland, which leads to the appearance in the following century of Evagoras I in the political sphere of Salamis. The *kouros* type is represented

Plate 104 by a small limestone head dating from the beginning of the fifth century, found during the excavations of the French expedition, and showing how successfully the Cypriote sculptor could render in limestone the nobility and beauty of the Greek sculpture of this period. The splendours of the city of Evagoras of the fifth and fourth centuries BC, which led the Greek orator Isokrates to praise it as the 'most Hellenic' of all the Greek cities, are still to be discovered. The coins of Evagoras, the abundance of Attic pottery including a Panathenaic amphora, and the quality of sculpture which the soil of Salamis has so far produced herald the architectural magnificence of its public buildings which one day must come to light. We need only mention a life-size marble head of a goddess, found built into an Early Christian wall in the Gymnasium, in 1952,[87] by way of example. The looped-up hair and noble facial features betray the early style of Praxitelean sculpture. This is certainly the work of a Greek sculptor working at the court of Evagoras, justifying most eloquently the information which we have from Isokrates that many prominent Greeks came to live at Salamis because they regarded the rule of Evagoras as more democratic than the political system of their own country.[88]

Plate 106

Plate 105

In the Hellenistic period under the Ptolemies, Salamis continued to be the largest city of the island though it ceded to Paphos its role of capital. Its original harbour must have begun to silt up and a new harbour some two miles farther north was constructed which, as we know, was used in 306 by Demetrius Poliorketes.[89] Remains of this harbour have been traced by divers during the last few years.

Probably as a result of this silting-up of the old harbour the city started shifting northwards, towards the new harbour, where new public buildings must have been constructed during the peaceful period which followed the re-establishment of the Ptolemies as rulers of Salamis and the whole of Cyprus from 294 until 58 BC. Evidence for such public building, a Gymnasium, was found in the northern sector of Salamis where the Department of Antiquities started excavations in 1952.[90] This evidence is both archaeological and epigraphic. A large part of a wall constructed of limestone ashlar was found at a depth of about two metres below the late Roman level of the Gymnasium. This building, associated with Hellenistic pottery, must have collapsed during the earthquakes which destroyed large areas of Salamis during the reign of Augustus. The debris of the earthquakes was compacted together with sand and stones, and thus the new Augustan Gymnasium was built on a much higher level, but on the solid foundations of the Hellenistic

Plates 107, 108

Salamis

Plate 122

Gymnasium, following at least the line of the latter's façade. Nothing else is known about the architecture of the Hellenistic Gymnasium. Its existence, however, is attested by inscriptions found within the area of the Gymnasium and mentioning athletic contests and Gymnasiarchs as early as the third century BC.[91]

Inscribed statue-bases of the Hellenistic period have been found in the area of the Gymnasium, where they must have originally stood. One of them is in honour of the strategos of the island, Helenos, and was dedicated by the secretariat of the Pancyprian guild of actors which was centred at Salamis.[92] This is interesting evidence for the importance of Salamis during the Hellenistic period (end of the second century BC), when the city must have retained its position as cultural centre of Cyprus despite the fact that Paphos became the administrative capital.

Of the Augustan Gymnasium substantial remains have survived and a few parts of its architectural plan may be reconstructed with a reasonable degree of accuracy. It consisted of a series of consecutive buildings running roughly from north to south, constructed of well-dressed sandstone blocks, with large niches in the walls which probably contained statues. There must have been three such rooms facing the front, two lateral rooms flanking a large central room. The length of the façade must have been about 50m. In front of it there was a Π-shaped colonnade of stone columns, the short sides of which measured 10m. Very little survives of the back rooms of the building, but walls of this period have been traced more than 50m. from the façade to the east. The Augustan Gymnasium must have contained a large bathing establishment, the main parts of which were incorporated into the baths of the second century AD which succeeded it. The pavement of the large stoa along the façade was of grey and white pebbles which have survived under the mosaic and marble floors of the Roman and Early Christian periods respectively.

There is no evidence for a colonnaded Palaestra in the Augustan Gymnasium. Most probably an open area covered with sand extended in front of the long portico of the façade. In fact trial trenches have revealed a thick layer of sand without any constructions in

101, 102 In a deposit, or ritual *bothros*, west of the city site of Salamis, excavated in 1968, a large number of limestone statuettes have been found, evidently belonging to a nearby sanctuary. The most usual type is that of a woman, wearing a chiton and himation and holding a flower in the right hand. The drapery is delicately treated and its folds recall Late Archaic Greek sculpture, especially the *korai* from the Acropolis of Athens (end of the sixth century BC). These statuettes, usually about 30 cm. high, bear traces of vivid colours both on their faces and on their drapery

103, 104 The period about 500 BC coincides with a revival of Hellenic ideals in Cyprus at a time when both Greece and Cyprus were facing the danger of Persian despotism. Greek styles in sculpture were very much in vogue in Cyprus and were often imitated by local artists in limestone; the prevalent types are the *kore*, *left*, found in the *bothros* near Salamis (as Plates 101, 102) and the *kouros*, exemplified by the beautiful head, *above*, found within the city site of Salamis by the French Expedition of the University of Lyon

105 The same Hellenic tradition continued in the island's sculpture in the fifth and fourth centuries BC. We know that Greek artists were working in the courts of the kings of Salamis, and this life-size marble head of a goddess (Aphrodite ?) may be the work of a Greek sculptor of the beginning of the fourth century BC. It was found in the Gymnasium of Salamis, where it was used in the Early Christian period as building material

106 Silver stater of King Evagoras I of Salamis (411–374 BC), representing on the obverse the head of bearded Heracles, the panhellenic hero, wearing the lion's skin; on the right border is the name of Evagoras in the Cypriote syllabary. The reverse of this stater shows a seated goat. (Enlarged × 10)

107, 108 At the northern sector of the city site of Salamis the Department of Antiquities of Cyprus has been excavating since 1952. About 100 metres from the seashore, within a forest of mimosas, a large area has now been cleared of the sand and débris which accumulated above the ruins since the abandonment of the site in the seventh century AD. A large group of public buildings dating from the Roman period down to this date has come to light, *above*. These include a spacious Gymnasium, with its colonnaded Palaestra and bathing establishment, *below*

109, 110 Very near the Gymnasium the remains of a theatre have been uncovered. This theatre, once one of the largest of the ancient world, was much destroyed, first by the earthquakes of the fourth century AD, and subsequently by stone-robbers. It had an auditorium with a capacity of about 15,000 spectators, and a large monumental stage. The diameter of the orchestra, originally paved with marble, was 27 m. This orchestra was screened off with a small wall during the Late Roman period, when the theatre was used for aquatic games (*naumachia*). The stage building was decorated with marble statues, several of which have been found among the débris, *left*; they are usually of second century AD date. The theatre has now been partially restored for theatrical and other cultural performances

111–113 The marble statues found in the débris of the *proskenion* of the theatre, unfortunately were all headless. *Above, left*, is a statue of Melpomene, the Muse of tragedy, holding a tragic mask in her left hand; *above*, a statue of Apollo Musagetes (leader of the Muses), who held a lyre in his left hand and wears a long chiton. Other statues found included Mnemosyne, the mother of the Muses, and it is not unlikely that there may have been a group of statues of all nine Muses and Apollo, decorating the façade of the stage building of the theatre. *Left*, the seated infant Herakles slays the snakes

114 The colonnaded Palaestra is the most monumental part of the Gymnasium. Its East Stoa is paved with marble tiles and must have been decorated once with marble statues, some of which were retained even during the Early Christian period. At the south and north ends of the East Stoa there is a swimming pool; round the north swimming pool several of the statues found in the course of the excavations have been erected to form an open-air sculpture gallery

115 The marble columns of the Palaestra were brought from the stage building of the nearby Theatre, at the time of the Early Christian reconstruction of the Baths of the Gymnasium, to replace the stone pillars of the Roman Gymnasium which were destroyed by the fourth century AD earthquakes. This is the reason why they differ in size. Their Corinthian capitals are of the third century AD, but they were re-used in the fifth century AD

116 At the south-west corner of the Palaestra of the Gymnasium are the latrines, forming a semi-circular colonnaded stoa in which there is seating for 44 persons. There was a perfect drainage system and sanitary installations in these latrines, which are the largest ever found in Cyprus

117 The upper half of a marble statue of Herakles of the Farnese type, of the second century AD. It was found in several pieces in a disused water tank of the Baths of the Gymnasium. This is a delicate piece of sculpture and may be considered as nearer to the Lysippian prototype than many other Roman copies of the same type

118 Marble head of a bearded man of the Antonine to Severan period, found behind the West Stoa of the Palaestra of the Gymnasium. This is a portrait head bearing some resemblance to Septimius Severus, though it cannot be definitely identified as that Emperor

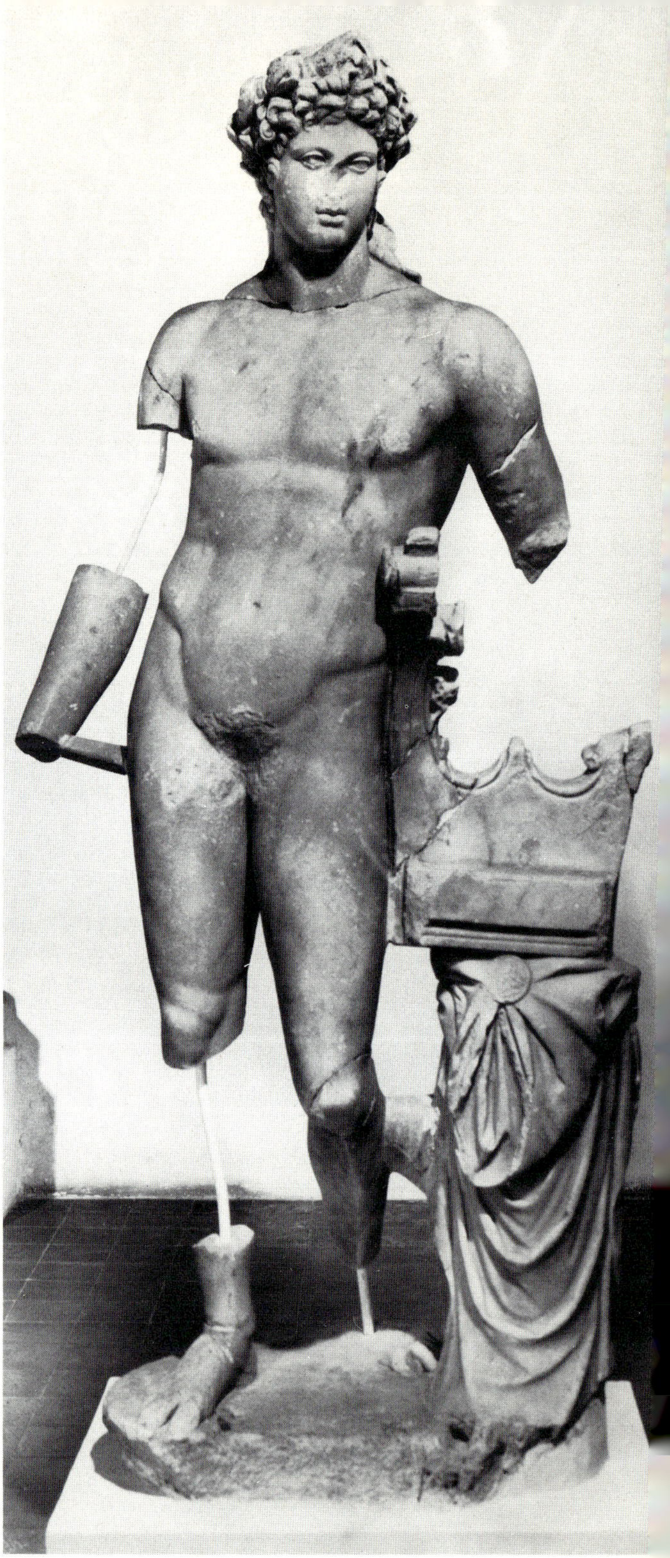

119, 120 Few marble statues with their heads on were found at Salamis, and among these are two over life-size statues of Hera, *left*, and of Apollo the lyre-player, *right*. The body of the former was found in 1890 in the Gymnasium and the head was found in 1958 near the temple of Zeus, a distance of about one mile apart. The statue of Apollo was found in numerous fragments in the north swimming pool of the East Stoa of the Gymnasium

121 Gem of chalcedony found in the Palaestra of the Gymnasium of Salamis. It represents a lion and bears the name of its engraver, Hyllos, which is known from other gems which he engraved. This gem is dated to the Early Roman Imperial period. (Enlarged × 5½)

122 An altar of marble found built into a late enclosure in the East Stoa of the Gymnasium. It is decorated with a garland in high relief, enclosing four masks, also in high relief, representing a Satyr, a Silenus, a Maenad or Ariadne and a Maenad or Dionysos. It bears an inscription in Greek stating that the altar was dedicated to Hermes by Diagoras son of Teucer, who was Gymnasiarch for life. It is not unlikely that this altar belonged originally to the orchestra of the Theatre and was removed to the Gymnasium together with other building material at the time of the Early Christian reconstruction. The imprints of a circular altar are still to be seen in the concrete cement of the floor of the orchestra

123, 124 Niches in the various bathrooms of the Gymnasium were decorated with polychrome wall-mosaics at the end of the third century AD. These were blocked with masonry during the Early Christian period, but the recent excavations brought to light again what survived of the wall-mosaics. A large niche in the south auditorium was decorated with a composition representing Apollo (in the centre) and Artemis (left) slaying the Niobids. Plate 124 shows a detail from the central part with the leg of kneeling Apollo above, his lyre, quiver and bow in the middle, and below a decorative garland with a female head in the centre

125, 126 *Left*, a headless, over life-size, statue of a winged Nemesis found in the East Stoa of the Gymnasium. With her right hand she pulls forward her drapery in order to spit in her chest, a characteristic gesture connected with her popular cult as Goddess of Jealousy. In her left hand she holds a measure, one of her attributes with which she measures the deeds of men. By her right foot is a griffin with one leg raised and resting on a wheel. *Right*, a headless life-size statue of a Spring Goddess found in the Palaestra of the Gymnasium. By her left foot is a support in the form of a rhyton, ending in a goat's head which served as a fountain. The 'wet' quality of the drapery supports her identification as a Water Divinity

127 Limestone statue of a *kore* found in a disused room behind the North Stoa of the Palaestra of the Gymnasium. This is an imitation by a Cypriote artist of a type which is specifically Greek, of the end of the sixth century BC

128 Statue of a female figure in grey marble, found near the swimming pool at the northern extremity of the East Stoa of the Palaestra. Its face, hands and feet were white marble insets and are now missing. This type is usually identified with Persephone, a mournful figure of Greek mythology, hence the grey colour of her drapery

this area. Finds dating to the Augustan period include a fine gem of chalcedony discovered in the area of the Palaestra; it represents a lion and bears the signature of its engraver, Hyllos.

An earthquake destroyed the city in AD 76/77, including the Gymnasium, which was rebuilt under the emperors Trajan and Hadrian. An inscription found embedded in the floor of the Early Christian period refers to the reconstruction by Trajan of the roof of a swimming pool of the Gymnasium which had collapsed. Hadrian also contributed to the cost of the embellishment of the Gymnasium, and several honorific decrees have been found which mention him as a 'benefactor of the city'. One of them was dedicated to him by the guild of the linen-weavers of Salamis.

The new Gymnasium was much larger than that of the Augustan period. Three colonnaded sides were added to the long side of the Augustan Π-shaped colonnade, and its short sides were abolished, resulting in a four-sided colonnaded portico which enclosed an open courtyard, a palaestra, in front of the Baths of the Gymnasium. The dimensions of this palaestra are 52.50m. east-west and 39.50m. north-south. Its columns were of white limestone and their shafts as well as their capitals were stuccoed. Several fragments of these have been found, and some bases were even re-used in an Early Christian reconstruction. The drums of the shafts from these columns were used as building material in the later reconstruction and many of them have been found, still retaining their dressing with stucco and reeded flutings. Two rectangular annexes with swimming pools were added at the north and south extremities of the large east stoa of the Palaestra. Their pools were originally elliptical, and had a small roofed portico running round three sides. It is the roof of one of these two swimming pools which Trajan restored after its collapse, according to the inscription already referred to. That the annexes may have been decorated with statues is suggested by some of the niches in their walls. The three rooms along the façade of the Augustan Gymnasium were retained, the large one in the centre being used as a sudatorium. It had two entrances, one at each corner by the back wall; the niches above these entrances were decorated with frescoes; that above the south entrance still retains parts of the original fresco decoration, depicting a well-known mythological scene: Hylas, the young friend of Herakles, who was sent to fetch water from a spring, is seen behind a hillock on the left, holding a spear in his right hand and raising his left arm as if to ward off the allurements of the nymphs with the open palm of his hand. At a lower level, a female figure, a nymph, extends her right arm towards Hylas. Water, rendered in blue, flows from the nymph's hand. The colours, green, brown, purple and blue, are preserved in all their vividness. The large black eyes of the young boy and his rich blond hair render his face very expressive and beautiful. Both the style of the painting and various external architectural criteria point to the end of the third century AD as a terminal date for this fresco.

The walls of the sudatorium were dressed with marble slabs up to a height of about two metres. Underneath the floor was a hypocaust, which was supplied with hot air by two large *praefurnia* lying at a depth of 2.50m. below the floor level, on either side (north and south) of the sudatorium. The large brick-lined channels which conducted the hot air from the praefurnia to the hypocaust have been found. The central part of the floor of this room was hollow and was filled with water which was heated by the hypocaust underneath, thus creating steam in the sudatorium where the bathers lay on couches on the raised benches around the four sides of this shallow pool.

On either side of this central sudatorium was a rectangular room with an octagonal (originally rectangular?) pool and with niches for statues round the walls. These two rooms were the frigidaria of the Baths. Their walls were dressed with marble, and there were two fountains in recesses.

A doorway in the middle of the back (east) wall led through a narrow corridor to the central sudatorium. The floor of this narrow passage was hollow and was partly heated so as to moderate the temperature for users of the Baths who proceeded from the frigidarium to the sudatorium and vice-versa. Two openings on the east wall of the sudatorium gave access to another large rectangular room, measuring 29m. × 13.70m., which has been identified as the caldarium of the baths. It had a hypocaust below its floor and a series of individual bathing basins, as well as a large semicircular one against an apsidal back (east) wall. Its roof, as well as that of the central sudatorium was in the form of a barrel-vault of large blocks of stone decorated with painted stucco. On the north wall of the caldarium (and probably also on the south wall, which was completely rebuilt at a later period) there were three niches high above the floor which were blocked with masonry during the Early Christian period, in order to cover their mosaic decoration. In one niche only a small part of the mosaic was found intact after the removal of the blocking masonry but in the second a substantial portion has been preserved. It is polychrome, with predominant red, yellow and green tesserae. It has a central medallion in a circle, now damaged, and on either side there are floral motifs and acanthuses. A human figure springs from the floral motifs on either side, of which one is more or less well preserved. The style of the composition, especially the acanthuses, recalls later Early Christian mosaics in the island (*e.g.* those from Kiti and Kanakaria) and the Salamis mosaic may be regarded as the closest forerunner of these. No mosaic was found in the third niche which had largely collapsed.

Along the north and south sides of the caldarium and behind the praefurnia, there were two large sudatoria with an apsidal façade facing the sea (east), in which were three openings (windows?). Thus the baths of the Gymnasium had a sea-side triple apsidal façade, with the central apse of the caldarium in the middle and the two apses of the lateral sudatoria on either side. It is too early yet to determine in detail the entrances to the various rooms from the outside because their excavation has not yet been completed and because of the extensive modifications made later to the architectural plan of the baths.

The north sudatorium is 29m. long and 10.9m. wide. Along its south wall there were two openings leading to the caldarium. Along its north wall, and high above the floor, a niche and an arch had been blocked in Early Christian times as in the case of those of the caldarium, in order to conceal pagan pictorial mosaics. Of the mosaic decoration in the niche a substantial part had survived, consisting of a wide horizontal band along its lower part, decorated in a beautiful polychromy with a garland of leaves, flowers and fruit (pomegranates). Above this horizontal band there must have been the main decoration of which only a small part of the background has survived. Unfortunately no traces have been found of the mosaic decorations of the arch.

The south sudatorium, also had one niche and two arches along its south wall, high above the floor level. Both arches were blocked up by later masonry. The large central niche was decorated with a large polychrome mosaic composition consisting of a decorative horizontal garland at its base, composed of leaves, flowers and fruit, with the head of a female figure (Flora?) in the centre. The main compositon depicts a mythological scene which has been identified as the slaying of the Niobids by Apollo and Artemis. Apollo, the central figure, has his left knee on a rock and his right leg is stretched out to the side; he has thrown his lyre on the ground by his feet and taken arrows from his quiver (shown in front of him); the upper part of his body is missing. Artemis, wearing a short chiton and sandals (the upper part of her body also is missing) runs to the left while another human figure on the right, wearing blue stockings and a mantle, leans against a pilaster with crossed legs, evidently looking on. No traces of the Niobids remain. The terminal date of this mosaic as well as of all the other wall mosaics of the baths is the end of the third century AD. The blocks of the niche were dislodged during the earthquakes of the fourth century AD, and this offers a good chronological guide. One of the two arches also contained a polychrome mosaic composition, part of which survived. It represents the old bearded river-god Evrotas, reclining with bare torso. In his left hand he holds a bough; with his right hand he touches his grey hair while his elbow is supported on an upturned jar from which water is flowing. He is looking right, towards a swan, of which one wing survives; above, Eros is seen flying towards the left; a wing and part of his body is preserved. The whole obviously represents the well-known legend of Zeus as a swan and Leda. The name of the river-god is written in white capital letters of the Greek alphabet against the black background of the composition which was enclosed within a rectangular frame filled with a guilloche pattern.

The wall-mosaics of the Salamis Gymnasium, in spite of their fragmentary condition, are of unique importance because mural mosaics from this period are rarely encountered, for the simple reason that usually the foundations only and not the whole walls of buildings survive from antiquity. There must also have been pavement mosaics at the Gymnasium of which there is evidence in the east stoa of the Palaestra, but this mosaic floor was completely destroyed during the Early Christian period, when it was replaced by a marble pavement, perhaps for the same reason that the wall mosaics had been concealed.

Not only the baths of the Gymnasium, as we have already mentioned, but also the porticos round the two swimming pools and round the Palaestra must have been decorated with marble statues, a large number of which have been found during the excavations. These represent gods and heroes of Greek mythology, and date mainly from the early second century AD; they may have been erected during the benevolent rule of either Trajan or Hadrian who were, as we know, lovers of the Greek culture. *Plates 117–120, 125, 126, 128*

Behind the south and north porticos the Gymnasium contained the various rooms that correspond to the standard plans of Roman Gymnasia as described by Vitruvius. Behind the west portico there was probably a street, access to which was gained through ten openings in its back wall. Beyond the south-west corner of the Palaestra were the latrines of the Gymnasium. They consisted of a semicircular portico inside which were 44 seats arranged round the back wall. There was a perfect system of sanitation, with water flowing constantly into the drainage as well as in a channel in front of the seats. Finally in front of the latrines there was a monumental fountain, separated from the rest of the building. *Plate 116*

The Palaestra itself was an open courtyard, with a circular pool in the centre. It had a floor of sand, as in the Augustan period. Finally, adjoining the Baths of the Gymnasium to the south-east, were two large vaulted water tanks for the supply of the large quantities of water needed for the baths, the swimming pools and the latrines of the Gymnasium. Water was conveyed to the various sections of the building by means of built channels and clay or lead pipes often hidden under pavements or behind walls. Large masonry sewers carried the effluent from these establishments to the sea.

The two earthquakes of the fourth century AD (332 and 342) which destroyed the city of Salamis and in fact all the ancient towns of Cyprus, caused the collapse of the Gymnasium, which must have been left abandoned, while the rest of the city was rebuilt as a Christian city under the name of Constantia, in honour of the Emperor Constantius II who assisted in its reconstruction.[93] After being deserted for a century the Gymnasium was partially restored, as baths for the new Christian city. The debris from the fourth-century AD earthquakes was cleared from the bathrooms behind the east portico as well as from the Palaestra and the porticos. A few of the rooms behind the south and north porticos were restored on a small scale, others were filled with debris. The frigidaria, the sudatoria and the caldarium of the baths were restored, some of their walls being completely rebuilt with the debris from the Roman Gymnasium, including the stuccoed stone walls of the Palaestra. The hypocausts were extensively repaired, the water supply system and the drainage. In several cases new water channels had to be built in the debris which was thrown outside the baths, at a level about one metre above the original ground level. The columns of the Palaestra were all replaced with marble columns and marble Corinthian capitals, most probably taken from the stage of the nearby theatre which was not fully restored after the earthquakes. There were eleven large columns along the east portico, seventeen columns and two pilasters of a smaller size along the long south and north colonnades, and thirteen columns and two pilasters along the west colonnade. Between the columns of the north, south and west colonnades the architrave was supported on arches which brought the roof of the corresponding porticos to the same height as the roof of the east portico with the large columns. In several instances the small columns of the three sides of the colonnade differed in size from one another, in which case bases of various heights were built so that the tops of the capitals (also of various styles and sizes) should be at the same level. The central pool of the Palaestra was built over with a stepped podium which carried a monument in the form of a doric column of grey marble; the steps also had a facing of grey marble. The southern half of the courtyard was paved with tiles but in the northern half only a foundation of stones was laid. The floor of the east portico was paved with marble tiles; these were removed from the orchestra of the theatre, as examination of the impressions left in the cement foundation of the latter showed. The annexes of the swimming pools on either side of the east portico were rebuilt, and smaller rectangular pools were built within the original elliptical ones.

Outside the baths, along the north and the south sudatoria, large arches were constructed to support the weakened outer walls of the building which, as evidenced by the fallen debris found during the excavation, must have had two storeys. On either side of the fountain in front of the latrines, a wall was built which screened them off from the Palaestra and the portico. Obviously, new conceptions were introduced with the new religion. Every attempt was made to obliterate pagan symbols; inscriptions were erased and the niches with mosaic compositions of pagan themes were blocked up. The fresco in the niche above the south door of the central sudatorium were plastered and an inscription was painted over, of which the word KYPIOY (of our Lord) survives. It may seem strange, however, that some of the statues of gods, especially those of Zeus, Asklepius, Apollo, and Nemesis, were tolerated, and after deliberate decapitation and mutilation, were left to adorn the baths. Yet this is not really surprising, if we consider that by the fifth century AD, Christianity was already the established official religion in Constantia. A number of other statues, namely nude Aphrodites, Hermaphrodites and Meleagers were, however, thrown into drains or into disused rooms behind the porticos. New latrines were built on a smaller scale than the old ones in a little room outside the baths, to the north, in a discreet corner of the building; this room was roofed and had a tiled floor. Finally, crosses were engraved on the columns and walls, confirming the triumph of the new religion. But even so, the Christian Salaminians were still proud of their glorious past. On the pavement of the east portico of the Palaestra a marble slab is engraved with an inscription praising an official of the city who, 'by his pious laws and good administration gave Cyprus its pristine glory'. The inscription, flanked with crosses, and written in elegiac metre with several mistakes in spelling, dates from the sixth century AD.

By reconstructing not only the Baths of the Gymnasium but also the buildings well outside the walls of Constantia, as we shall see, Constantius II restored the whole of Salamis to its former size, though only the central part of it was fortified with a city wall. The new Christian city regained its premier place among the other cities of Cyprus as the island's religious and administrative metropolis.

Then came the Arab invasions of AD 647–8, to deal Salamis a final blow. The city was pillaged and in the end a fire destroyed it completely.[94] The burnt surface of the walls of the Gymnasium bear eloquent witness to the final disaster which caused the gradual abandonment of Salamis about seventeen centuries after its foundation. Its inhabitants fled to the south and founded medieval Famagusta. Squatters must have occupied the Gymnasium for a number of years after its destruction. In the meantime, however, blown sand carried from the beach by north-easterly winds accumulated within the ruins of the Gymnasium and finally covered them up completely. But even this was not the end. Stone robbers in medieval times must have been active in this area of the ruined city and the existence of two kilns for gypsum within the area of the Gymnasium is indicative of the manner in which the marble statues and architectural components of this building must have perished in order to make good quality gypsum.

The excavation of the Gymnasium, which is not yet complete, has not only revealed a fine monument, but has also thrown light on the history of Salamis during the late period of its existence. It has demonstrated the importance and wealth of the city during the Roman period. The size of this building, its lavish decoration with numerous marble statues, and the information which is supplied by inscriptions about the cultural and social life of the city, show

*The City Site*

how it retained its place as the leading cultural centre of Cyprus throughout its history. The fact that out of the numerous inscriptions found within the area of the Gymnasium only one or two were in Latin, all others being in Greek, testifies that even under Roman rule this city continued its Greek tradition.

At a site about 100m. south of the Gymnasium, which was previously occupied by late Hellenistic houses, lies the Theatre of Salamis. Its excavation, started in 1959, has not yet been completed, but its general architectural plan is known. It was completely covered by debris and sand and planted over with mimosas; only a slight hollow in the ground betrayed its existence.

Stratigraphical study suggests that it must have been built in the time of Augustus. It follows the architectural scheme of the Roman theatres in Asia Minor, and does not differ much from that of Aspendos, though it is less well preserved. Its auditorium, built on flat ground, faces west, and the spectators thus sat with their backs to the sea. One of the major pagan public buildings near the Baths of the Gymnasium destroyed by the fourth-century AD earthquakes, it suffered by being used as a quarry to provide building material for the Early Christian reconstructions of the Baths in the fifth century AD.

The Theatre has an orchestra slightly larger than a semicircle with a diameter of 27m., a criterion for the large size of the original edifice. It was paved with variously coloured marble slabs within rectangular panels; these slabs, however, were removed in order to pave the east stoa of the Palaestra of the Gymnasium, as was ascertained by comparing the designs of the panels in the latter with impressions left in the cement in the orchestra. In the centre of the latter there is a hollow circular space for an altar. In fact we found a marble altar of the same diameter in the eastern stoa of the Gymnasium, bearing an inscription which is a dedication to Hermes by the Gymnasiarch for life called Diagoras son of Teucer. The orchestra was screened from the auditorium by a low parapet wall and a passage for the spectators which also had openings for rainwater to run into drains below. The stage runs parallel to the diameter of the orchestra, in front of the auditorium; the actual

Plate 122

proscenium had a length of about 40m. and a depth of 5m., and there was a floor supported on colonnettes of stone at a height of 2m. above the level of the orchestra. Its wooden planks rested on the front wall of the proscenium at one end, and at the other they were fixed in rectangular sockets at the base of the wall of the massive frons scenae. This, following the models of theatres of Asia Minor, runs parallel to the diameter of the orchestra, with rectangular recesses which must have been flanked with columns and may have contained statues and honorific inscriptions. There are the usual three doors which lead through the frons scenae to the platform of the proscenium, but of the actual façade of the frons scenae only the foundations have survived. The parascenia on either side of the proscenium and the other stage buildings behind the frons scenae have still to be excavated.

The inner half of the auditorium was supported on a solid base of masonry, but the outer half, beyond the diazoma (now missing) rested on a complicated system of radiating walls with superimposed arches. Only the foundations of these survive, together with the massive outside wall of the theatre which is 3.80m. thick. By projecting the vertical line of the outer wall and the oblique line of the existing seats of the auditorium, we arrive at 20m. as the approximate original height of the latter, which may have provided for more than 50 rows of seats, accommodating about 15,000 spectators. Of the seats, only the foundations of the eight lower rows have survived and the actual seats of the last two rows, which were of white limestone, moulded in the usual fashion of theatre seats. Above the sixth row of seats was a rectangular recess for the thrones of the city officials, but none of these has survived. The parodoi at either end of the auditorium were paved with limestone slabs. Halfway along them there were steps leading up to the diazoma, of which only the lower ones survive.

From the time of the erection of the Theatre to the time of its destruction by earthquakes in the fourth century AD, it underwent several modifications. Some time in the third century AD the orchestra was completely screened off from the auditorium and the parodoi by a parapet wall all round it about one metre high, thus forming with the front wall of the proscenium a semicircular pool which was filled with water for aquatic games.

At either end of the diameter of the orchestra there is a cylindrical statue base, formerly a funerary cippus of the Hellenistic period. These bases bear inscriptions in honour of Marcus Aurelius Commodus and the Caesars Constantius and Maximianus respectively.

The earthquakes of the fourth century AD caused the collapse of the arched substructure of the auditorium as well as the façade of the frons scenae. Large parts of walls are still lying as they fell at the time of the earthquakes. The pillars, statues and honorific inscriptions of the frons scenae also fell and were covered by the debris, to be found in a fragmentary condition during the excavations. Most of the statues represent Muses such as Mnemosyne and Melpomene; there is one of Apollo Musegetes and two others of cuirassed emperors. The quality of the statues recalls the schools of sculpture of Asia Minor along the Ionian coast or of Aphrodisias in Caria. It is worth mentioning again that the Salamis Theatre is based on prototypes in Asia Minor, such as those at Ephesus, Perge, Miletus, Side and Aspendus. Most of the statues from the Theatre, as well as those from the Gymnasium, date from the second century AD. They must have been made during the reign of Hadrian (AD 117–138) who restored peace in the island after the troubled period of the Jewish revolt in AD 116. It is not surprising, therefore that in one honorific inscription, from the debris of the proscenium of the theatre, Hadrian is hailed as 'Benefactor of the Salaminians and Saviour of the World'.

Plates 110, 113

Plates 111, 112

We have already referred to the systematic robbing of the stone blocks and columns of the Theatre at the time of the Early Christian reconstruction of the near-by Baths of the Gymnasium. In spite of that, however, there is evidence that during the Early Christian period, probably in the sixth century AD, the stage was restored on a much smaller scale and by utilizing those seats of the auditorium which had not collapsed, the derelict Theatre was used for mimic productions, as was the custom in Constantinople and elsewhere.

All round its outer wall, and between radiating walls of the substructure of the auditorium, squatters built houses, mostly of timber. These were burnt down at the time of the Arab invasions, surviving now in the form of thick layers of ashes and charcoal above the debris of the fourth-century earthquakes.

At the theatre have been found a number of inscriptions mentioning a wealthy citizen of Salamis, Servius Sulpicius Pancles Veranianus, who lived during the Flavian period. They record that he, *inter alia*, restored the statues of the Gymnasium (probably after the earthquakes of AD 76–77) and repaired the amphitheatre 'which is between the theatre and the gymnasium'. This amphitheatre has in fact been located there. The blown sand which shrouded it was removed, but debris still covers its walls and seats, awaiting its turn to be excavated. The walls of its elliptical perimeter, about two metres thick, still rise to a considerable height.

# VI

# Salamis—Constantia

We have already stressed the fact that after the earthquakes of the fourth century AD the new city of Constantia was rebuilt on a very large scale, equal in extent to its Roman predecessor. Only a small part, however, at the centre of the city, was walled; this wall may date from the seventh century AD, and have been built in an attempt to defend the heart of the city from the Arab raids. It has rectangular towers at regular intervals and was built of material from earlier ruined buildings, such as drums of stone columns. One of the major public buildings enclosed by it is the Basilica excavated in 1924–25 and 1954–58 by the Department of Antiquities.[95] This excavation however, is still to be completed. The construction of the basilica, which became the metropolitan church of Constantia, was initiated by St Epiphanius who occupied the See from AD 368 to 403. It is the largest known basilica on Cyprus (58m. long and 42m. wide) and must have been an imposing building with three aisles on either side of the central nave from which they were separated by stone columns, 14 on each side, carrying large Corinthian capitals.

At the eastern extremity of the central aisle of the three on the southern side an empty tomb was found, the sides of which were lined with marble, and which may well have been that of St Epiphanius. We know, however, that his relics were removed to Constantinople by the Emperor Leo the Wise (AD 886–912).

East of this tomb a large annexe of the Basilica was converted into a church, after the Arab invasions which started in 647 and during which Muawiya profaned the original basilica. This new church must have continued in existence during the Middle Ages.

Another magnificent building of the Early Christian period has come to light in the last three years during the excavations of the French Mission.[96] It consists of a large colonnaded rectangular courtyard with porticos on all four sides, adjoining a three-aisled basilica on the west. Two corridors to the north and south connect the west courtyard with another colonnaded courtyard east of the basilica. The models for such a complex should be sought in the East rather than in Greece and Asia Minor. Throughout its history the appearance of Eastern architectural elements is not an uncommon phenomenon in the architecture of Salamis, side by side with Greek architectural inspiration.

At this site, known as Cambanopetra, there is evidence of the continued occupation of Salamis-Constantia during the Medieval period, at a time when Famagusta to the south was already a prosperous city. Coins of the Lusignan period, found both here and in the area of the Basilica of St Epiphanius bring the history of Salamis down to the thirteenth century AD thus giving the city site a life of twenty-three centuries, from the time of its foundation in the eleventh century BC down to its final abandonment.

Salamis has thus become the major archaeological site of Cyprus, with a diversity of ancient remains of extraordinary interest and great monumentality. In the preliminary report of the British expedition of 1890 the leader wrote in 1891: 'Italy has her Herculaneum and Pompeii; why should not Cyprus, and through Cyprus England, give to the world a *Salamis rediviva?*'[97] It is no exaggeration to claim that this dream is now being fulfilled, with Salamis becoming one of the most important ancient sites in the Mediterranean.

# Notes

## Foreword

1 Two volumes have already appeared: V. Karageorghis, *Sculptures from Salamis* I, 1964; V. Karageorghis and C. C. Vermeule, *Sculptures from Salamis* II, 1966.
2 One volume has already been published: V. Karageorghis, *Excavations in the Necropolis of Salamis* I, 1967. The second volume is in preparation.
3 Preliminary reports on each year's excavations have appeared regularly in *Bulletin de Correspondance Hellénique* (since 1958), *Archaeological Reports* and elsewhere. For an up-to-date bibliography, see *Sculptures from Salamis* I and II.

## Chapter I

4 See C. F. A. Schaeffer, *Enkomi-Alasia* I, Paris 1952.
5 For recent general accounts on Salamis (especially the early periods) in the light of new archaeological research see: J. Pouilloux, 'Salamine de Chypre: le site et ses problèmes', *Comptes Rendus, Académie des Inscriptions et Belles Lettres* (1966) 232 ff.; M. Calvet, 'Une Tombe du XIe siècle av. J.-C. à Salamine de Chypre', *ibid.* 348 ff.; for a history of Classical Salamis, based mainly on literary, epigraphic and numismatic evidence, see C. Spyridakis, Κύπριοι Βασιλεῖς τοῦ 4ου αἰ. π.Χ. (411–311/10 π.Χ.), Nicosia 1963.
6 There are frequent references to Salamis in ancient Greek authors, mainly in connection with the role it played in Greek politics in the fifth and fourth centuries BC. Herodotus describes the part played by Salamis and its kings in the wars against the Persians, mainly in the Ionian revolt (see references in Gjerstad, *op. cit.*, 471 ff.). Isokrates in one of his orations (Πρός Νικοκλέα) praises the most famous of the Salaminian Kings, Evagoras I.
7 For a general account on the history and archaeology of Cyprus during the eighth and seventh centuries BC and especially the role of kingship in the development of Cypriote culture during

this period, see E. Gjerstad, *The Swedish Cyprus Expedition*, vol. IV, part 2, 1948, 449 ff.
8 For a recent study of the subject with a general account in the position of Cyprus between the Aegean and the Near East, see J. Boardman, *The Greeks Overseas*, Harmondsworth, 1964, mainly pp. 57 ff.
9 D. G. Hogarth, *Devia Cypria*, 61.
10 L. Palma di Cesnola, *Cyprus, its ancient cities, tombs and temples*, 202.
11 A. Palma di Cesnola, *Salaminia*, xxii.
12 See *Sculptures from Salamis* II, 10 ff.
13 See *Mitteilungen des Deutschen Archäologischen Insituts, Athenische Abteilung* 6 (1881), 191–208, and 245–255; 8 (1883), 133–140; see also Salomon Reinach, *Chroniques d'Orient* I (1885), 179–184.
14 See D. M. Bailey, *Opuscula Atheniensia* VI (1965), 5 ff.
15 See *Journal of Hellenic Studies* XII (1891), 59–198.
16 See A. H. Murray and others, *Excavations in Cyprus*, 1 ff.
17 For references, see *Sculptures from Salamis* II, 9 f.
18 Preliminary reports have been published in the *Journal of Hellenic Studies* and *Archaeological Reports*, and since 1958 in the *Bulletin de Correspondance Hellénique*.
19 See note 5 above.

## Chapter II

20 For the colonization of Salamis by Teucer and the problems involved, see E. Gjerstad, 'The Colonization of Cyprus in Greek legend', *Opuscula Archaeologica* III (1944), 108 ff.
21 The name of a Teucrian is recorded on an altar of the Roman period found in the Gymnasium of Salamis (*Sculptures from Salamis* I, pl. XXXVIII).
22 See G. A. Wainwright, 'A Teucrian at Salamis in Cyprus', *Journal of Hellenic Studies* 83 (1963), 146 ff.
23 See note 5 above.
24 *Cf.* Schaeffer, *Enkomi-Alasia* I, 315 ff.
25 See note 20 above.

## Chapter III

26 See note 7 above.
27 *Cf.* R. D. Barnett, *A Catalogue of the Nimrud Ivories in the British Museum*, London, 1957, 60 ff.

28 Cf. J. Boardman, *The Greeks Overseas*, 57 ff.
29 For a further discussion on the connections between Euboea and Cyprus, see V. Karageorghis and L. Kahil, *Antike Kunst* 10 (1967), 133 ff.
30 A. H. Murray and others, *Excavations in Cyprus*, 1 ff.
31 The results of this excavation have been published by P. Dikaios in *Archäologischer Anzeiger* 1963, 126 ff.
32 Cf. the *Iliad* XXIII, 243, *Archäologischer Anzeiger* 1963, 147 f., and *Bulletin de Correspondance Hellénique* 91 (1967), 244 f.
33 For a general discussion on horse-burials, see V. Karageorghis, *Excavations in the Necropolis of Salamis* I, 117 ff. and *idem*, *Archaeology* 18 (1965), 282 ff.
34 For references to Homeric burial customs in connection with those studied in the necropolis of Salamis, see V. Karageorghis in *Stasinos* I (1963) 33 ff., and more recently 'Homerica from Salamis', *Europa* (Festschrift E. Grumach, Berlin 1967), 167 ff.; see also M. Andronikos, 'Totenkult', *Archaeologia Homerica* 85.
35 The results of this excavation have been fully published in *Excavations in the Necropolis of Salamis* I, 6 ff.
36 For slave burials, see *ibid.*, 121; the same custom has been observed in a recently excavated tomb at another site of the Salamis necropolis (Cellarka) as will be seen below (p. 132).
37 See *ibid.*, 118 f.
38 See *ibid.*, 124 ff.
39 For a study of such decorated metal bowls from Cyprus, see E. Gjerstad in *Opuscula Archaeologica* IV (1946), 1 ff.
40 This tomb has been published in detail in *Excavations in the Necropolis of Salamis* I, 74 ff.
41 Ivory blinkers are referred to in the *Mycenaean Linear B tablets from Knossos* (*Nestor* 1 March 1966, 429); Homer also refers to ivory blinkers in the *Iliad* IV, 140 ff.
42 For references to earlier literature about this monument, see *Excavations in the Necropolis of Salamis* I, 90 ff., where also the results of the recent excavations are discussed in detail.
43 See *Archaeologia* 66 (1915), 171 ff. and 159 ff. respectively.
44 Published in detail in *Excavations in the Necropolis of Salamis* I, 25 ff.
45 Cf. *ibid.*, appendix IV, 133 ff.
46 See V. Karageoghis in *Europa*, 167 f.
47 See *Excavations in the Necropolis of Salamis* I, 43 and fig. 11.
48 Cf. *ibid.*, 46 ff.

49 *Cf. ibid.*, appendix IV, 132; also *Kadmos* 1965, 147 ff.
50 *Cf. Excavations in the Necropolis of Salamis* I, 121 f.
51 Published in detail, *ibid.*, 54 ff.
52 For the occurrence of cremation as a method of burial at Salamis see *ibid.*, 119 ff.
53 Preliminary reports have appeared in the *Bulletin de Correspondance Hellénique* 91 (1967), 337 ff.; *Illustrated London News*, 16 Dec. 1967, 26 ff.
54 It recalls the funerary chariots represented on the Greek Geometric (Dipylon) amphorae, and the εὔπλεκτοι or εὐπλεκεῖς δίφροι of Homer (*Iliad* XXIII, 335, 436). See also *Europa*, 170.
55 For representations of Ishtar on horses' gear, see R. D. Barnett, 'North Syrian and related harness decoration', *Vorderasiatische Archäologie* (Berlin, 1964), 21 ff.; M. L. Barrelet, 'Les déesses armées et ailées', *Syria* 32 (1955), 222 ff., and H. Kantor, 'A bronze plaque with relief decoration from Tell Tainat', *Journal of Near Eastern Studies* 21 (1962), 93 ff.
56 Horses' gear in ivory of more or less the same period decorated with very similar representations have been found at Nimrud. See J. J. Orchard, *Equestrian Bridle-Harness Ornaments*, London, 1967, pl. XX ff.
57 For a study of such cauldrons, see recently H. V. Hermann, *Die Kessel der orientalischen Zeit*, Olympische Forschungen VI, Berlin, 1966; see also R. Maxwell-Hyslop, *Iraq* 18 (1956), 156 ff.; U. Janzen, *Archäologischer Anzeiger* (1966), 123 ff.; J. Benson, *Antike Kunst* 2 (1960), 58 ff.
58 For references to recent discussion on the significance of fire dogs, see *Bulletin de Correspondance Hellénique* 87 (1963), 292 ff.
59 See recent discussion by the present writer in *Archaeologia Homerica*, 99 ff.
60 See *Kadmos* (1967), 98 f.
61 See M. E. L. Mallowan, *Nimrud and its Remains* II, 485 ff.
62 See *Archaeologia Homerica*, 100 ff. and *Europa*, 168 ff. Ivory chairs and stools decorated with blue paste (Κύανος) and gold are described in the Mycenaean Linear B tablets from Pylos. See M. Ventris and J. Chadwick, *Documents in Mycenaean Greek*, Cambridge, 1956, 343 ff.
63 Mallowan, *op. cit.*, 512.
64 For almost identical ivory plaques, *cf.* Crowfoot, *Early Ivories from Samaria*, London, 1938, pl. II, 2.
65 *Cf.* Mallowan, *op. cit.*, fig. 479.

66 Cf. D. B. Harden, *The Phoenicians*, London, 1962, pl. 15.
67 Cf. Mallowan, *op. cit.*, p. 409, fig. 335.
68 Cf. *Bulletin de Correspondance Hellénique* 91 (1967), 286 n. 6, fig. 26.
69 For metallic Phoenician jugs of this type, see D. B. Harden, *The Phoenicians*, pl. 53.
70 Cf. Rodney Young, 'Late Geometric graves and a seventh century well in the Agora', *Hesperia Supplement* II, 1939, 19ff.
71 Cf. Kathleen Kenyon, *Jericho* I, London, 1960, pl. VII, 3.
72 Cf. Ch. Picard, *Les religions préhelléniques*, Paris, 1948, 208f.
73 Cf. Boardman, *The Greeks Overseas*, 65.
74 Cf. *Bulletin de Correspondance Hellénique* 92 (1968), 328.
75 Cf. *Kadmos* (1965), 150.
76 Cf. Herodotus, *Histories*, V, 104, 108–115; G. F. Hill, *A History of Cyprus* I, 118ff.
77 Cf. *Bulletin de Correspondance Hellénique* 90 (1966), 373ff.
78 Cf. *Clara Rhodos* III, 146ff.
79 Hill, *op. cit.*, 167.

## Chapter IV

80 L. Palma di Cesnola, *Cyprus, its ancient cities, tombs and temples*, 202.
81 A. H. Murray, and others, *Excavations in Cyprus*, 1.
82 Cf. Pausanias VII 18, 11–13; cf. also references to other monuments (pyramid tombs) of Anatolia in *Bulletin de Correspondance Hellénique* 90 (1967), 328 n. 2.
83 Emile Kunze, *VI. Bericht über die Ausgrabungen in Olympia*, Berlin 1958, pl. 12ff.
84 See Hill, *op. cit.*, 160f.

## Chapter V

85 *Journal of Hellenic Studies* XII (1891), 146ff.
86 V. Karageorghis, *Sculptures from Salamis* I, pl. VII.
87 *Ibid.*, pl. VIII–IX.
88 Isokrates, *Evagoras*, 21.
89 Cf. Hill, *op. cit.*, 168.
90 For a short account on the recent excavations at the city site of Salamis, see *Sculptures from Salamis* I, 1ff.
91 Cf. J. Pouilloux, 'Les trois Gymnases de Salamine de Chypre', *Revue Archéologique* 2 (1966), 337ff.

92 See T. B. Mitford, 'Helenos, Governor of Cyprus', *Journal of Hellenic Studies* 79 (1959), 100f.
93 *Cf.* Hill, *op. cit.*, 245.
94 *Ibid.*, 285.

## Chapter VI

95 For preliminary reports on these excavations, see *Journal of Hellenic Studies*, from 1954 onwards.
96 For preliminary reports, see *Bulletin de Correspondance Hellénique* 92 (1968), 322ff.
97 *Journal of Hellenic Studies* XII (1891), 121.

# Select Bibliography

CALVET, M. 'Une tombe du XIe siècle av. J.-C. à Salamine de Chypre', *Comptes Rendus, Academie des Inscriptions et Belles Lettres* 1966, pp. 348–53.

CESNOLA, A. PALMA DI. *Salaminia (Cyprus). The History, Treasures and Antiquities of Salamis in the Island of Cyprus.* London, 1882 (2nd ed. 1884).

CESNOLA, L. PALMA DI. *Cyprus.* London, 1877.

DIKAIOS, P. 'A Royal Tomb at Salamis, Cyprus', *Archäologischer Anzeiger* 1963, pp. 126–208.

GJERSTAD, E. 'The Colonization of Cyprus in Greek Legend', *Opuscula Archaeologica* III (1944), pp. 107–23.

—— *The Swedish Cyprus Expedition*, IV (2), Stockholm, 1948.

HILL, SIR GEORGE. *Catalogue of the Greek Coins of Cyprus.* London, 1904, pp. 46–65.

—— *A History of Cyprus* I. Cambridge, 1940.

HOGARTH, D. G. *Devia Cypria. Notes on an Archaeological Journey in Cyprus in 1888.* London, 1889.

JEFFERY, G. E. 'The Basilica of Constantia, Cyprus', *Antiquaries Journal* VIII (1928), pp. 344–9.

—— 'Rock-cutting and Tomb-Architecture in Cyprus during the Graeco-Roman Occupation', *Archaeologia* LXVI (1915), p. 159 ff.

—— *The Ruins of Salamis.* Nicosia, 1946.

KARAGEORGHIS, V. Yearly preliminary reports on the excavations at Salamis in the *Bulletin de Correspondance Hellènique* since 1958.

—— 'Ten Years of Archaeology in Cyprus 1953–62', *Archäologischer Anzeiger* 1963, pp. 579–94.

—— (with the collaboration of Cornelius C. Vermeule). *Sculptures from Salamis* I. Nicosia, 1964.

—— with O. MASSON. 'Quelques Vases inscrits de Salamine de Chypre', *Kadmos* 4 (1965), pp. 146–53.

—— and C. C. VERMEULE. *Sculptures from Salamis* II. Nicosia, 1966.

—— 'Recent discoveries at Salamis (Cyprus)', *Archäologischer*

*Anzeiger* 1966, pp. 210–55.

—— *Excavations in the Necropolis of Salamis* I. Nicosia, 1967.

—— 'Die Elfenbein-Throne von Salamis, Zypern', *Archaeologia Homerica* 1968, pp. 99–103.

—— *Cyprus*. Geneva, 1968.

MASSON, O. *Inscriptions Chypriotes Syllabiques* (Études Chypriotes I). Paris, 1961, pp. 318–23.

MITFORD, T. B. 'Helenos, Governor of Cyprus', *Journal of Hellenic Studies* 79 (1959), pp. 94–131.

MUNRO, J. A. R. and TUBBS, H. A. 'Excavation in Cyprus 1890. Third Season's Work, Salamis'. *Journal of Hellenic Studies* 12 (1891), pp. 59–198.

MURRAY, A. H., SMITH, A. H. and WALTERS, H. B. *Excavations in Cyprus*. London, 1900, p. 1 ff.

MYRES, J. L. 'Notes on the "Prison of Saint Catherine" at Salamis in Cyprus', *Archaeologia* LXVI (1915), pp. 179–94.

OBERHUMMER, E. 'Salaminia, Salaminiae Insulae, Salamis', *Paulys-Wissowa Real-Encyclopadie*. Stuttgart.

OHNEFALSCH-RICHTER, M. 'A Prehistoric Building at Salamis', *Journal of Hellenic Studies* 4 (1883), pp. 111–16.

POUILLOUX, J. 'Salamine de Chypre: le site et ses problemes', *Comptes Rendus, Académie des Inscriptions et Belles Lettres* 1966, pp. 232–56.

—— 'Les trois Gymnases de Salamine de Chypre. Note sur une inscription retrouvée', *Revue Archéologique* 1966, pp. 337–40.

REINACH, S. *Chroniques d'Orient de 1883 à 1890*. Paris, 1891.

SPYRIDAKIS, K. *Euagoras I von Salamis*. Stuttgart, 1935.

ΣΠΥΡΙΔΑΚΙ, Κ. Κύπριοι Βασιλεῖς τοῦ 4ου αἰ. π.Χ. (411–311/10 π.Χ.). (Ἑταιρεία Κυπριακῶν Σπουδῶν, I). Λευκωσία, 1963.

TAYLOR, J. du P. 'A Water-cistern with Byzantine Paintings, Salamis, Cyprus', *Antiquaries Journal* XIII (1933), pp. 97–108.

# List of Illustrations

Unless otherwise acknowledged illustrations are by courtesy of the Department of Antiquities, Cyprus. The objects are in the National Museum of Antiquities, Nicosia, Cyprus.

## Colour Plates
AFTER PAGE 64
- I Bronze cauldrons in the dromos of Tomb 79.
- II Chariot Δ with two horses in the dromos of Tomb 79.
- III Detail of the head of one of the horses of chariot Δ with its gear *in situ*.

AFTER PAGE 82
- IV Ivory lotus flower plaque from the ivory throne in Tomb 79. Ht 16cm.
- V Ivory sphinx plaque from the ivory throne in Tomb 79. Ht 16cm.
- VI Ivory throne from Tomb 79. Ht 90cm.
- VII Ivory plaque with the god Heh from Tomb 79. Ht 7cm.
- VIII Ivory plaque with confronted sphinxes from Tomb 79. Ht 7cm.
- IX Painted clay bowl and stem with figures from Tomb 47. Ht 36cm.
- X Stemmed bowl decorated in polychrome from Tomb 23. Ht 23cm.

AFTER PAGE 156
- XI Tumulus 77 after excavation.
- XII Clay head on the pyre in Tumulus 77.
- XIII Detail of the pyre in Tumulus 77.
- XIV Gilded and painted clay alabastra from the pyre in Tumulus 77. Average ht 23cm.
- XV Clay portrait head from the pyre in Tumulus 77. Ht 17.5cm.
- XVI Clay head of a male figure from the pyre in Tumulus 77. Ht 29cm.
- XVII Wall mosaic of Evrotas in the Gymnasium.

## Monochrome Plates
AFTER PAGE 32
1. Proto-White Painted ware jug from an eleventh century BC tomb at Salamis. Excavations of the Université Lyon, Institut F. Courby.
2. Proto-White Painted ware bowl from the same tomb as 1.
3. Detail from a Proto-White Painted ware bowl from the same tomb as 1.
4. Necklace of gold and rock-crystal beads. Tomb 1.
5. Imported Attic geometric crater. Tomb 1. Ht 48cm.
6. Excavations in dromos of Tomb 1.
7. Façade and burial chamber of Tomb 1.
8. Impressions of a wooden chariot in the floor of the dromos of Tomb 1.
9. Façade and burial chamber of Tomb 2.
10. Skeleton of an ass in the dromos of Tomb 2.
11. Bronze blinkers from an ass. Tomb 2. L. left 19.5cm., right 17.5cm.
12. Head of an ass *in situ* with its gear in the dromos of Tomb 2.
13. Ivory blinkers from a horse. Tomb. 47. L. 16cm.
14. Bronze frontal band from a horse. Tomb 47. L. 38cm.
15. Scarab of Osorkon I. Tomb 47. Base 1.8 × 1.3cm.; ht 0.8cm.
16. Dromos and burial chamber of Tomb 47.
17. Two horse skeletons. First burial, Tomb 47.
18. Six horse skeletons. Second burial, Tomb 47.
19. Vaulted chamber of Tomb 50 before excavation.
20. Interior of the chamber of Tomb 50.
21. Dromos and vaulted chamber of Tomb 50 after excavation.
22. Two horse skeletons. Tomb 50.
23. Stone façade and built dromos wall of Tomb 3.
24. Detail of amphora with inscription. Tomb. 3.
25. Iron sword. Tomb 3. L. 92cm.
26. Bronze banner from the yoke of a chariot. Tomb 3. Ht 54cm.
27. Chariot group in repoussé on a gold diadem. Tomb 31. L. 9cm.
28. Amphora with incinerated remains. Tomb. 31.
29. Dromos and burial chamber of Tomb 31.
30. Asses on the floor of the dromos of Tomb 31.
31. Three legged jar. Tomb 31. Ht 31cm.
32. Bird-shaped askos. Tomb 31. L. 18cm.

# Salamis

AFTER PAGE 100

33 Dromos and façade of the burial chamber of Tomb 79.
34 Rear view of burial chamber and dromos of Tomb 79.
35 Pottery in the dromos of Tomb 79.
36 Soil impression of chariot B. Tomb 79.
37, 38 Bronze head of a lion from hearse Γ. Tomb 79. Ht 11.5cm.
39 Hearse Γ. Tomb 79.
40 Bronze cauldrons in the dromos of Tomb 79.
41 Pottery in the larger cauldron in the dromos of Tomb 79.
42 Ivory chair near the façade of Tomb 79.
43 Ivory 'incense-burner'. Tomb 79. Ht 31cm.
44 Ivory leg of a stool or table. Tomb 79. Ht 36.5cm.
45, 46 Bronze lynch pin from chariot B. Tomb 79. Ht 37 and 19cm.
47 Iron knife with ivory handle. Tomb 79. L. 36.5cm.
48 Bronze horse blinker with repoussé El. Tomb 79. L. 47cm.
49 Bronze side pendant with repoussé Ishtar. Tomb 79. L. 53cm.
50 Murex shells from the dromos of Tomb 79. Shell top left, 22cm.
51, 52 Pair of iron fire-dogs. Tomb 79. L. 110cm.
53 Bundle of iron obeloi. Tomb 79. L. 150cm.
54 Hydria. Tomb 79. Ht 42cm.
55, 56 Amphorae. Tomb 79. Ht 105 and 110cm.
57 Painted decoration on interior roof of Tomb 80.
58 Built façade and roof of Tomb 80.
59 Detail of Pyre L, Cellarka.
60 Clay rosettes from Pyre L, Cellarka.
61 Clay incense burner. Pyre A, Cellarka. Ht 25.5cm.
62 Engraved bone. Pyre A, Cellarka. Ht 13cm.
63 Clay arm wearing a bracelet. Pyre AE, Cellarka. L. 22cm.
64–68 Pottery from Tomb 105, Cellarka. Ht 98, 18, 145, 10.5, and 27cm respectively.
69 Interior of Tomb 105, Cellarka.
70 Dromos and façade of Tomb 84, Cellarka.
71 Carved stomion of Tomb 84, Cellarka.

AFTER PAGE 132

72 Tomb 6, Cellarka, with infant burials.
73 Jars with infant burials above Tomb 7, Cellarka.
74–76 Terracotta figures. Tomb 27A, Cellarka. Ht 7.5, 8, and 7cm. respectively.
77 Standing terracotta figurine. Tomb 85A, Cellarka. Ht 13.5cm.
78 Seated terracotta figurine. Tomb 41, Cellarka. L. 9cm.
79 Terracotta figurine of a man in a boat. Tomb 104, Cellarka. L. 11cm.
80 Bezel of a finger ring. Tomb 73, Cellarka. L. 1.7cm.
81 Clay shield. Tomb 13, Cellarka. Diam. 23cm.
82 Proto-Attic amphora. Tomb 84, Cellarka. Ht 88cm.
83 Skyphos imitating Greek prototypes. Tomb 23, Cellarka. Ht 10cm.
84 Rhodian bowl. Tomb 29, Cellarka. Ht 4.5cm.
85 Tumulus 77 before excavation.
86 Tumulus 77 after excavation.
87 Pyre in the centre of the exedra. Tumulus 77.
88 Gold rosettes from the pyre. Tumulus 77. Largest diam. 2cm.
89 Iron spear-heads from the pyre. Tumulus 77. Top left, L. 18cm.
90 The exedra dug across. Tumulus 77.
91 Carbonized wood in post-hole. Tumulus 77.
92 Clay portrait head from the pyre. Tumulus 77. Ht 15.5cm.
93 Clay female head from the pyre. Tumulus 77. Ht 27.5cm.
94 Clay horse's head from the pyre. Tumulus 77. L. 19cm.
95 Clay breast of a female figure from the pyre. Tumulus 77. Ht 21cm.
96 Back of clay male head from the pyre. Tumulus 77. Ht 29cm.
97 Clay feet of human figures from the pyre. Tumulus 77. Largest foot, L. 20.5cm.
98, 99 Shield from the pyre and reconstructed drawing. Tumulus 77.
100 Iron arm-band of a shield from the pyre. Tumulus 77. L. 33cm.

AFTER PAGE 168

101–103 Three limestone kouroi from a *bothros* of a sanctuary near St Barnabas. Ht 43, 29, and 35cm. respectively.
104 Limestone head of a kouros, south sector of city site. Ht 10.5cm. Excavations of the Université Lyon, Institut F. Courby.
105 Marble head of Aphrodite from the Gymnasium. Ht 31cm.
106 Silver stater of Evagoras I, king of Salamis.
107 Aerial view of the northern sector of Salamis.
108 Aerial view of the Gymnasium.
109 Aerial view of the Theatre.
110 Statues found in the debris of the stage building of the Theatre.
111 Statue of the muse Melpomene from the Theatre. Ht 94cm.
112 Statue of Apollo Kitharodos from the Theatre. Ht 105cm.
113 Statue of the infant Heracles from the Theatre. Ht 35.5cm.
114 East stoa of the Gymnasium, from the south.
115 West colonnade of the Palaestra of the Gymnasium, from the south.
116 Latrines of the Palaestra of the Gymnasium.
117 Marble statue of Heracles from the Gymnasium. Ht 72cm.
118 Marble male head from the Gymnasium. Ht 26cm.
119 Marble statue of Hera from the Gymnasium. Ht 217cm.
120 Marble statue of Apollo from the Gymnasium. Ht 203cm.
121 Intaglio signed by the engraver Hyllos from the Gymnasium. L. 2.5cm.

*List of Illustrations*

122 Marble altar from the Gymnasium. Ht 113cm.
123, 124 Wall mosaic from the baths in the Gymnasium.
125 Statue of Nemesis from the Gymnasium. Ht 182cm.
126 Statue of a nymph from the Gymnasium. Ht 121cm.
127 Archaic kore from the Gymnasium. Ht 74cm.
128 Statue of Persephone from the Gymnasium. Ht 130cm.

## Figures

The plans and sections are the work of the Surveyor, Antiquities Department, Cyprus; figures 20–27 are by Jane Cook.

1 Plan of the site of ancient Salamis, p. 15.
2, 3 Sections of Tomb 2, pp. 28–29.
4 Plan of Tomb 2, p. 30.
5 Plan of Tomb 47, p. 51.
6 Horses of the first burial, Tomb 47, p. 52.
7 Horses of the second burial, Tomb 47, p. 55.
8 Plan of Tomb 50, Period I, reconstructed, pp. 56–57.
9 Section of Tomb 50, Period I, reconstructed, pp. 56–57.
10 Horses from Tomb 50, p. 59.
11 Section of Tomb 50, Periods I–IV, pp. 60–61.
12 Plan of the chamber, Tomb 50, Periods I, II and III, p. 60.
13 Plan of the chamber, Tomb 50, Periods I–IV, p. 61.
14 Plan of Tomb 50, Periods I and II, pp. 62–63.
15 Plan of Tomb 3, pp. 68–69.
16 Plan of Tomb 19, p. 73.
17 Plan of upper levels with later surface graves, Tomb 31, pp. 74–75.
18 Plan of Tomb 31, pp. 74–75.
19 Section of Tomb 31, pp. 76–77.
20 Repoussé disc with winged lion and enemy, Tomb 79, p. 79.
21 Bronze side pendant ornament with repoussé beetle, Tomb 79, p. 85.
22 Breast-plate with mythical figures, Tomb 79, p. 86.
23 Head band with lions, uraei, human figures, Tomb 79, p. 87.
24 Head band with figure of the god El, Tomb 79, p. 87.
25 Blinker with a lion attacking a bull, Tomb 79, p. 88.
26 Blinker with a winged sphinx and Negro, Tomb 79, p. 88.
27 Bronze cauldrons in the dromos, Tomb 79, p. 91.
28 Plan of the chamber tombs at the Cellarka site, pp. 118–119.
29 Plan of Tomb 105, Cellarka, pp. 122–123.
30 Section of Tomb 105, Cellarka, pp. 124–125.
31 Plan of Tomb 84, Cellarka, p. 126.
32 Plan of Tomb 10, Cellarka, pp. 128–129.
33 Plan and section of Tomb 23, Cellarka, p. 131.

# Index

*Numbers in italics refer to the plates*

Abdemon, 149
Achilles, 8
Aeschylos, 20
Agamemnon, 8
Ajax, 7
Alexander the Great, 155f.
Alexandria, 154
Al Mina, 24, 127
Arab invasions, 16, 192, 196f.
Argos, 91
Assyrian domination, 14, 23, 25, 94, 98
Athens, 7
Augustan period, 167ff.
Axiothea, 164

Barnabas, St, and Monastery of, 18, 25, 54, 166
Basilicas, Early Christian, 197f.
Bronze Age Salamis, 20–22

Cambanopetra, 198
Catherine, St, 54, 63; *19–22*
cauldrons, bronze, 89ff.; *40, 41, 1*
Cellarka, site of, 99–150; *59–79*
cenotaph, 10, 151ff.; *85–100, XI–XVI*
Cesnola brothers, 17, 151
chariots, 9, 27, 68f., 78ff.; *8, 27, 36, II*
Constantia, 190ff., 197f.
Constantius II, Emperor, 190, 192
cremation, 8ff., 26, 73, 119f.; *30*

Demetrius Poliorketes, 167
Diagoras son of Teucer, 193; *122*
Dikaios, Dr P., 7, 25
Dorians, 10

Egyptians, 14
Enkomi, Bronze Age city, 13f., 20ff., 72, 152
Epiphanius, St, 197f.

Eretria, 24
Etruria, 90
Evagoras I, 14, 18, 166f.; *106*
Evelthon, 99
excavations at Salamis (before 1952), 17f., 25, 54f., 67f., 151

Famagusta, 7, 13, 16f., 192
fire-dogs, 91f.; *51, 52*
furniture, ivory, 10, 24, 82, 92ff.; *42–44, IV–VIII*

Greek colonization of the Near East, 10, 24, 26, 127, 149
Greek pottery, 24, 26, 128ff., 132; *5, 82, 84*
Gymnasium of Salamis, 16, 25, 167ff.; *107, 108, 114–116*

Hadrian, 185, 189, 195
hearses, 9, 32, 53, 70, 80f., 85; *37–39*
Herakles, 186; *113, 117*
*heroon*, 62
Homeric burial customs, 7f., 12, 26f., 71
Homeric epics, 7, 70f., 92
horse and ass burials, 9, 27, 31f., 53f., 57f., 72f., 78, 129f.; *10, 12, 16–18, 22, 29, 30, II, III*; gear, 27, 31f., 53f., 70f., 79, 85ff.; *11, 13, 14, 48, 49*
human sacrifices, 9, 30f., 132
Hylas, 186

infant burials, 119f., 128, 149f.; *72, 73*
inhumation, 8f., 27, 98, 120
Isokrates, 18, 166

Jewish revolt, 195

Kition, 21, 23
*kollyva*, 121

Lapithos, 31
Lusignans, 16, 198
Lysippos, 155, 156, 163

Mycenaeans, 8, 13f.

Nicocreon, 10, 12, 156, 163f.
Nimrud, 94, 96

Ohnefalsch-Richter, Dr M., 18, 54, 76, 79, 99
Olympia, 154
Osorkon I, 54; *15*
Oxus Treasure, 70

Palaepaphos, 27, 91
Paphos, 167
Patras, altar of Artemis Lafria, 153
Patroklos, 8f., 27, 31f., 71
Pausanias, 153
Penelope's throne, 10, 94
Persians, 14, 132
Phoenicians, 12, 23f., 50, 149
Pindar, 20
Pouilloux, Professor J., 20
Proto-White Painted ware pottery, 21; *2*
Ptolemy, 10, 163, 167
pyres, 8, 12, 26, 117ff., 127, 153ff.; *59, 87, XII, XIII*

Ramesses III, 20

Salamenski, 20
Sargon II, 23
sculpture from Salamis, 166f., 191, 195; *92–97, 101–105, 111–113, 117–120, 125–128*
Sea-Peoples, 20
Sidonians, 50
silver bowl from Tomb 2, 49f.
silver-studded sword from Tomb 3, 70; *25*

211

*Salamis*

Soloi, 128

Tamassos, 27, 31
Tarsus, 24
Telamon, 7, 20
Teucer, 7, 20 ff.
Theatre of Salamis, 16, 25, 193 ff.; *109, 110*
*tholos* tombs, 8
tin-plated pottery, 32, 54, 97, 127; *41*
Tomb I (French Expedition), 21 f.; *1–5*
Tomb 1, 25–28; *6–8*
Tomb 2, 28–50; *9–12*
Tomb 3, 67–72; *23–26*
Tomb 10, 128 f.
Tombs 19 and 31, 72–75; *27–32*
Tomb 23, 130 f.; *83*, X
Tomb 47, 50–54; *16–18*
Tomb 50 (Prison of St Catherine), 54–63, 99; *19–22*
Tomb 79, 76–98; *33–56*, I–VIII
Tomb 80, 98 f.; *57, 58*
Tomb 84, 127 f.; *70, 71, 82*
Tomb 105, 121–126; *64–69*
topography of Salamis, 13, 16, 165

Trajan, 185, 189
Trojan War, 7 f., 21
tumuli, 71 f., 151 f.; *85, 86*, XI

University of London (Institute of Archaeology), 49
University of Lyon (Institut F. Courby), 19 f., 165 f.

Vouni Palace, 31

wall mosaics, 161, 187 ff.; XVII